"Teaching is relentless, sapping, intense, and so many are feeling the pressures of workload, lack of appreciation, and begging to leave. Peter Foster writes from inside-the-classroom-out about how to resist the pull to conform, maximize feelings of control, become part of an effective team, share the love of improvement, how to reengineer the workload, prioritize the effective, and slow down and do less, better. It reads like a great novel, touches on dilemmas we all face, and is so positive about de-implementing, reengineering, and recapturing the joys of why we become teachers – to have a great impact on the learning lives of our students."

John Hattie, *Melbourne Laureate Professor Emeritus*

"This is a truly remarkable book. Peter has explored the reasons why so many teachers are ground down by unproductive processes that don't add value to learning. Things like potty non-negotiables, cumbersome processes, inconsistent communication from leaders. He also explores how it's possible to have colleagues buzzing about their work when the nonsense is stripped away. He talks from his own experience, from talking with colleagues and he underpins this with well-sourced research. And best of all, Peter provides a way of framing the challenges so that anyone working in a setting where sensible, human-centred practices are not the norm has the capacity to identify and address those areas that will make teaching more manageable, more enjoyable and more sustainable."

Mary Myatt, *Education writer and thinker*

"Many books look to address the complex array of challenges that teachers and leaders face. Only the best books manage to articulate easy to identify with, granular problems, and then skilfully lead the reader through clear, sustainable, practical solutions. If you want to improve your practice, if you are a leader wanting to support teachers or if you love teaching but are thinking about whether this exhilarating but intense profession is really right for you, then pause, take a moment, and have a look. This book is written for you!"

Dave Tushingham, *Co-author of* The Edu-book Club

"Peter explores the persistent challenges that teachers and leaders face and offers lots of practical guidance and tips on how these challenges can be navigated. With very clever use of vignettes, Peter is able to illustrate how these challenges play out in our day to day lives as educators and offers eminently sensible solutions in an easy-to-digest way. I found myself nodding along at so much of the book and I'm so glad some of these very knotty challenges have been addressed in this brilliant book. A must-read!"

Lekha Sharma, *School Improvement Lead, Avanti Schools Trust*

"Teaching is a rewarding profession, yet the current stressful landscape has contributed to an increasing number leaving the field. *The Long Game* by Peter Foster, emerges as a beacon of practical wisdom, addressing the very real struggles of teaching with a rare blend of empathy and expertise. Foster's writing style is not only readable but also deeply personable, making the journey through each page feel like a conversation with a wise mentor.

One of the book's core strengths lies in its examination of the myriad challenges teachers face in today's schools. From sustaining motivation amidst external pressures to the critical issue of managing an ever-increasing workload, *The Long Game* leaves no stone unturned. Yet, Foster approaches these problems with solutions that are balanced, thoughtful, and grounded in reality. This truly sets the book apart.

The Long Game is replete with realistic scenarios that accurately represent the experiences of teachers. Through these scenarios, Foster not only illustrates the challenges but dissects them while providing practical solutions.

The Long Game is a must-read for teachers of all levels but particularly for school leaders. A truly empowering read, this book is a testament to the resilience and dedication of teachers everywhere, and successfully provides the blueprint for a sustainable and rewarding teaching experience."

Dr Jo Castelino, *Curriculum Leader for Science*

"In the current recruitment and retention crisis, this book is crucial reading for all teachers and school leaders. Peter combines research evidence with personal reflections and others' experiences, to address the main causes of teachers leaving the profession and what school leaders and teachers themselves, might be able to do to address this. A really interesting and important book."

Jade Pearce, *Trust lead for professional learning*

"Lots of books about teaching tell us about new strategies or what we should be doing to improve our practice. This book is different. It tackles the thorny issue of teacher sustainability head on, with a myriad of practical strategies. For those of us who have just been told to 'work smarter!' Peter offers much more realistic and evidence-informed solutions, each explained with case studies and examples. It's the book I wished I'd had much earlier in my career to arm me to cope with the workload, time and immense energy needed to be an effective teacher. A must-read for teachers and leaders at all stages."

Rachel Ball, *Coaching Development Lead, StepLab*

"This is an honest, courageous and forthright exploration of what can overwhelm us and adversely affect our motivation as teachers – and what we, and those who lead us, can do about it. Peter Foster's new book is full of positive, practical and accessible examples: "real stories from real teachers", including insights from Peter's own experience which he openly shares. It is enriched by his wide reading and deep understanding of evidence-informed practice, and it offers suggestions from Peter, and from a range of serving teachers and leaders, about the strategies which can be useful as we step up to the challenges he describes.

At the end of each chapter he addresses how middle and senior leaders can support teachers and enable them to face the complex demands of their profession. Peter's consideration of the dynamic between leaders and members of their teams, and how we can make this as constructive and productive as possible, is full of insight and balanced good sense, for example his compelling advice about how teachers can feed back to leaders in a way which should help schools move forward more positively. I completely endorse his conviction that getting leadership (at all levels) right is crucial, if teachers are to thrive.

This book has much to offer classroom teachers, of any level of experience and in any setting, and those who lead them. I recommend it wholeheartedly."

Jill Berry, *Former head, now leadership development consultant*

"*The Long Game* offers an honest, refreshing and raw take on teaching. Whilst it starts off by looking at many of the issues that we all universally face in this profession the book then opens up with a wave of positivity and infectious enthusiasm for a career that is truly magical. *The Long Game* will ask you to consider that all important why question; namely why did you become a teacher and what is your moral purpose. A fantastic read and astutely timed to help energise colleagues when the narrative around teaching is one of doom and gloom. Bravo!"

Sam Strickland, *Principal, author, and educational speaker*

"By writing *The Long Game* Peter has tried to distill the very essence of what makes teaching so rewarding and demanding into a practical guide for how we can all make our lives a little easier and therefore more sustainable. By covering a broad range of topics including pedagogy and personal belief structures readers will be able to find specific advice to change the way they work or perceive their work to ensure they are less stressed and more effective. Using honest and real accounts of scenarios that real teachers have faced, the book is grounded in pragmatism and never once preaches to the reader. The extra guidance and reflective questions for leaders are particularly useful as they give leaders space to consider how they can create a school that supports teachers to flourish in the long term."

Adam Robbins, *Author of* Middle Leadership Mastery

"Teaching can be a challenging and sometimes arduous long game, but it is also one of the few careers that can change children's lives, and even change the world for the better. It is a job that matters and it is a job that is worth the effort. In Peter

Foster's new book, *The Long Game*, he exposes the flaws in seeking out silver bullet fixes and easy solutions, and instead presents a compelling alternative full of sustainable solutions for busy teachers. The book is jam-packed with practical solutions and well-crafted reflective steps. It offers the tools and insights to help make you think and thrive in the teaching profession."

Alex Quigley, *Head of Content and Engagement at the Education Endowment Foundation*

"There are many persistent challenges facing our wonderful profession; Peter sensitively but pragmatically outlines the difficulties of the job, and provides a comprehensive blend of research, case studies, and practical strategies to help all teachers and school leaders to thrive (and stay!) in their roles. From factors that influence motivation, to working efficiently, to building powerful working habits, there is an incredible amount to reflect on and then implement. We have a moral imperative to aid the flourishing of our teachers, and Peter takes on the challenge with knowledge, understanding, empathy, and a huge body of useful ideas."

Sam Crome, *Author of* The Power of Teams

"Teachers are the decisive element in ensuring pupils receive the education they deserve and yet schools are in the midst of a significant recruitment and retention crisis. *The Long Game* is a timely contribution to the solutions we need to ensure that schools are replete with highly motivated and effective teachers.

In this book, Peter Foster draws on the latest research from psychology and education to exemplify a way of working that balances the demands of workload and accountability whilst guarding against teacher burnout.

While we may often hear vague advice to 'work smarter', this book describes with absolute clarity what this might mean for busy teachers across the sector. By implementing the recommendations within, we are likely to not only improve the working lives of teachers but also enhance children's experiences of school.

Highly recommended."

Andrew Percival, *Deputy Headteacher at Stanley Road Primary School, Oldham*

"This book gets real about the challenges of being a teacher today – and offers us meaningful ways through these challenges. Peter shares with us, in an engaging, humble and down-to-earth way, his own story, bringing in those of others to add rich extra dimensions and drawing upon a rich and fascinating array of research to work out what's behind the challenges – and, most importantly, what we can do about it. Whilst he doesn't pretend it's easy, the result is that he represents our profession as a rich and rewarding one – and one worth sticking with for the long game! It contains a huge amount of valuable advice for teachers new and longer in tooth and is highly recommended to all those wanting to make this noble and challenging profession work for them."

Dr Emma Kell, *Teacher, coach, writer, and speaker*

"It's almost a cliché in education that every teacher has an escape plan for leaving the profession. In *The Long Game*, Foster has written a book that is both honest and chock full of insights into how teachers can regain a sense of purpose and motivation. No matter what side of the pond you teach on, this book will help teachers to find joy amid the constraints and to focus on what got us into this crazy labor of love in the first place. For me, it was to make a difference in the lives of young people. What's yours?"

Dr Zach Groshell, *Host of* Progressively Incorrect *podcast*

"While there is currently – and rightly – a great deal of focus on recruiting new teachers, we have thought less about how we keep the ones we already have. Likely many of us entering the profession didn't think far beyond surviving the first year, let alone sustaining our motivation for a life-long career.

In this brilliantly practical book, Peter offers thoughtful, highly applicable strategies to help busy teachers manage the complexity and intensity of the job, and retain their enthusiasm to do it well – to play 'the long game'. It is an invaluable guide for all teachers – a manifesto for making our profession one where teachers can thrive and – crucially – want to stay."

Sam Gibbs, *Trust Lead for Curriculum and Development,*
Greater Manchester Education Trust

The Long Game

Why do some teachers stay in teaching? And why do others leave? Why do some enjoy it whilst others find it an unrelenting slog? Answers to these questions are elusive but vital for new teachers, school leaders and everyone in between. Using research from wide-ranging fields and experience from real teachers, *The Long Game* examines how teachers can sustain and enjoy successful careers in teaching.

Divided into five parts, the book explores the persistent challenges of being a teacher by breaking them down into problems and solutions. The chapters unpack the factors that get in the way of our success or enjoyment of teaching and considers the different ways these problems can be tackled, addressing key concerns, including:

- How to maintain motivation *as you juggle work and life*
- How to manage intensity *in a non-stop job*
- How to embed effective, long-lasting habits *to save time and mental effort*
- How to reduce workload *not just 'manage' it*
- How to teach successfully and have impact *in a way that lasts*

Teaching isn't like a game because it is frivolous or simple. But it is an infinitely layered problem we can spend our careers trying to solve. To sustain a successful and enjoyable career in teaching, we need to embed strategies and approaches that will minimise the challenges and maximise our enjoyment. *The Long Game* will help teachers to hold onto the joy in teaching by facing the challenges head on.

Peter Foster is a teacher and school leader. He has worked in state comprehensives since qualifying as an English teacher in 2010. Peter currently works to support and develop teachers across a multi-academy trust in the South-West of England.

The Long Game

Sustaining a Successful Career in Teaching

Peter Foster

Routledge
Taylor & Francis Group

LONDON AND NEW YORK

Designed cover image: © Klaus Vedfelt / Getty Images

First published 2025
by Routledge
4 Park Square, Milton Park, Abingdon, Oxon OX14 4RN

and by Routledge
605 Third Avenue, New York, NY 10158

Routledge is an imprint of the Taylor & Francis Group, an informa business

British Library Cataloguing-in-Publication Data
A catalogue record for this book is available from the British Library

Library of Congress Cataloging-in-Publication Data
Names: Foster, Peter, 1951- author.
Title: The long game : how to sustain a successful career in teaching /
Peter Foster.
Description: Abingdon, Oxon ; New York, NY : Routledge, 2025. | Includes
bibliographical references and index.
Identifiers: LCCN 2024035864 (print) | LCCN 2024035865 (ebook) |
ISBN 9781032591384 (hardback) | ISBN 9781032591353 (paperback) |
ISBN 9781003453154 (ebook)
Subjects: LCSH: Teaching--Vocational guidance. | Teachers--Job satisfaction. |
Teachers--Workload. | Career development.
Classification: LCC LB1775 .F665 2025 (print) | LCC LB1775 (ebook) |
DDC 371.10023--dc23/eng/20241022
LC record available at https://lccn.loc.gov/2024035864
LC ebook record available at https://lccn.loc.gov/2024035865

ISBN: 978-1-032-59138-4 (hbk)
ISBN: 978-1-032-59135-3 (pbk)
ISBN: 978-1-003-45315-4 (ebk)

DOI: 10.4324/9781003453154

Typeset in Melior
by SPi Technologies India Pvt Ltd (Straive)

Contents

Part 3: Embedding Habits

Part 4: Reducing Workload

Part 5: Ensuring Success

Acknowledgements

I'm indebted to the teachers and leaders of Bridgwater and Taunton College Trust for their wisdom and experience. I learn an incredible amount working with such an incredible bunch of teachers every day. I'm particularly thankful to those teachers who were so generous with their time, sharing their experience inside and outside the classroom.

More colleagues than I can name here supported the writing of this book by reading chapters, challenging the ideas, and making suggestions. To everyone who helped me in this way, thank you.

Annamarie Kino and the team at Routledge have done a fantastic job of refining and improving my original plan for the book and the draft as it developed. Their insights have been invaluable.

This book would not exist without my dad. He's brought common sense to an initial reading, ironing out my bad writing habits. But more than that, he got me into thinking about what it means to work sensibly and well.

Alison, Isabelle, and Emilia – thank you for your patience and love.

Foreword

Legendary colleagues,

Effective teaching is important. It's probably the biggest lever we have at our disposal to improve the learning and life chances of the young people in our care (and safeguard the future of our precious society).

However, securing effective teaching, particularly at scale, is not easy. For several reasons... one of the biggest of which is that teaching is actually really complex. One of the most cognitively (and emotionally) demanding jobs ever invented.

And YET... this complexity is vastly under-appreciated. Largely because almost every adult has spent many hundreds of hours sat in classrooms, and (here's the kicker)... the better the teacher is, the easier they make it look (aka the 'paradox of teacher expertise').

As a result of this complexity under-appreciation, the role of the teacher has expanded, to the point where the job is at risk of being unsustainable. Where the system is at risk of haemorrhaging good, smart people who WANT to teach, but just can't square the toll it takes on their life.

Btw, there's an irony in all of this too... teachers exist to make people's lives better—it would be deeply incongruent to pursue this end in a way that made their own lives worse.

And so, for these reasons and more, I am OVER THE MOON that Peter has invested his mind and energies in helping us to better understand and begin to chip away at this problem... the problem of *making teaching sustainable*... perhaps the biggest problem of our era (beyond teacher effectiveness). And that he's doing it with an eye for rigour and bravery. Which is vital, because there are many ways that this work can go wrong, and a certain undertone of stoicism is required to get it right.

Peter—thank you for writing this book. Everyone else—let's join Peter in putting our minds and shoulders to the broader task of making teaching sustainable. It's unlikely to be a quick fix, but as a profession, we've already proved that we're not afraid of a challenge.

Enjoy the long game.

Peps Mccrea

Introduction

I'm not one of those people who wanted to be a teacher from a very early age. I never really knew I wanted to do it until I was in front of a class. I enjoyed it. I enjoyed the individual interactions that make up each lesson. I enjoyed the process of distilling subject content I'd spent years studying into hour-long manageable chunks. I enjoyed being at the front of the room and being quite comfortable there.

Teaching has been, since then, an enjoyable challenge. This book is about the challenges that define teaching, its deep problems, and what we can do to keep them in check.

The Persistent Challenges of *Being a Teacher*

A career in teaching is one spent encountering and overcoming challenges. Some of those are expected and repeated: behaviour and planning. Others are rare but thorny: a complaint from a parent. Others still are intractable and lingering: the question of how (and whether) education has the power to address the problems of deprivation, poverty, or inequality.

Mary Kennedy, a brilliant thinker on teacher development, wrote a seminal paper on the persistent problems of teaching.[1] These are the problems that we will always face as we try to make learning happen in the classroom. Kennedy's problems are

- Portraying the curriculum

- Enlisting student participation

- Exposing student thinking

- Containing student behaviour

- Accommodating personal needs

You can see the brilliance in Kennedy's summary of teaching. The problems are simple. We can understand what she means right away, but we can spend a career

DOI: 10.4324/9781003453154-1

I

trying to refine our solutions to these problems. Whilst I don't think Kennedy's list is incomplete, I do think there's another angle on such persistent challenges. We have, from Kennedy, the persistent problems of *teaching*, but we could, in addition, define the persistent challenges of *being a teacher*. The distinction is subtle but important.

Teachers need to come to work and excel in the face of Kennedy's problems, every day. To get to the point of being successful, we need to solve a deeper set of challenges. If left unsolved, these challenges will likely put a limit on what we can achieve.

In this list of challenges, I would include

- **Sustaining motivation** – When you start out in teaching, the *why* of teaching generally feels clear. As time passes, that clarity of purpose can wane in the face of arcane administrative practices and unrealistic accountability measures. Whilst it might be natural for new teachers to lose their early idealism, sustaining motivation to teach – to alter life chances of young people, to share love of subject, to develop skills and knowledge – is vital for a fulfilling career. To do this, we need to understand what motivates us, what can drain that motivation, and what we can do about it.

- **Managing intensity** – Teaching is more intense than many other jobs.[2] Intensity isn't simply about workload. From the moment the children arrive until a while after they leave, time to pause or rest is limited. Not only that, busy teaching days are a physical and emotional battle. How we manage that intensity will affect how we feel about teaching but also how much we get done each day. The more intensely we rip through each day, the less able we are to stop, reflect, prioritise, and think.

- **Embedding habits** – Time is not on our side. We have thousands of decisions to make each day. If we don't automate effective processes or embed positive routines, we could find our ability to attend to any number of important situations drown in our inability to focus.

- **Reducing workload** – *Managing* workload feels like settling for something. It feels like an admission that levels of work will never improve. To be really effective, we can't just *manage* endless work; we need to make room for the right kinds of work, the activities that will have the most impact on the most students. To do this, we'll need to cut and remove unhelpful practices.

- **Ensuring Success** – Success is a great motivator. We won't sustain a career without experiencing success, but what success looks like is often in the eye of the beholder. To some, success is career advancement. To others, it's the individual stories of student achievement. Part of this challenge is defining for ourselves what success will look like. But this can't be an entirely subjective process. We need to look at what it means to be an effective teacher and how that is possible each day.

Often workload alone is characterised as *the* problem of teaching, but this isn't quite right. What saps the enjoyment from teaching isn't simply that there is a lot to do. It is about the amount *and* type of work. It is the feeling that *my* work, it's quantity and type, aren't entirely within *my* control. It is the feeling that if I had more time and more space to think, I'd be able to improve what I do and how I do it. It's the danger of losing our motivation to teach, because what motivates us has been forced to the periphery.

Equally, behaviour does not feature overtly in my list, although it hovers behind and within several of these problems. The intensity of the day, our workload, our feelings of success, and motivation to teach, all of these are at times mediated by how well our class is behaving (or isn't). Our *persistent challenges of being a teacher* don't cover every aspect of a teacher's day or week. Instead, our challenges help and equip us to persist and succeed as a teacher no matter what those days or weeks present us with.

The Long Game in Summary

Each section of this book will deal with one of our persistent challenges of *being a teacher*. Within each section, chapters break down the challenges listed above into problems for us to solve. Each chapter is split into two main sections: *Problems* and *Solutions*. In *Problems*, we'll unpack what's getting in the way of our success or enjoyment of teaching. In *Solutions*, we'll consider different ways we can tackle the problem.

At the end of each section, there are some suggestions for middle and senior leaders, addressing how they can support teachers to face these challenges. These suggestions are signposted as *For Leaders*, but anyone can read them and consider how we can make schools the kinds of places where teachers can thrive.

This book can be read from start to finish, or you can use the information below to select the problems most relevant to you.

Before Part 1, the first chapter deals with how we select solutions that will help us in the long game.

Part 1. Sustaining motivation

In this section, we'll look at what gets in the way of our motivation to teach. If you're struggling with motivation and aren't sure why, you'll find solutions here.

Problems	Solutions
Chapter 2 Lack of autonomy increases stress levels and negatively impacts wellbeing.	Maximise feelings of control and push back against autonomy-sapping practices.

(Continued)

Problems	Solutions
Chapter 3 Teaching is an isolating profession.	Become an even more effective team member.
Chapter 4 When our development stalls, so does our motivation.	Commit to sustainable improvement.
Sustaining Motivation – Notes for Leaders	

Part 2. Managing intensity

Every teacher knows that teaching is intense, but how to manage that intensity can prove difficult. If you get to the end of a day, week, or term and feel completely drained, this section will offer potential reasons why as well as some solutions.

Problems	Solutions
Chapter 5 We have to process an overwhelming quantity of information each day.	Develop systems for managing information, messages, and tasks.
Chapter 6 A teaching day is physically and mentally exhausting.	Slow down and do less, better.
Managing Intensity – Notes for Leaders	

Part 3. Embedding habits

If you know you need or want to change your behaviour – in or out of the class-room – this section is for you. Behaviour change is hard; you'll find solutions here to make it more straightforward.

Problems	Solutions
Chapter 7 We can't force ourselves into behaviours that are more effective.	Develop a practice habit.
Chapter 8 Over time, we embed sub-par habits.	Replace existing habits with ones that are more effective.
Automating Process – Notes for Leaders	

Part 4. Reducing workload

This section looks at the impact of workload, how we can manage it effectively but also reduce it. If it feels like the work never stops, if you're not sure what to do, or if you want to do less, we'll examine some solutions here.

Problems	Solutions
Chapter 9 We have to manage large quantities of work in a finite amount of time.	We must become experts in organising our time.
Chapter 10 The quantity expected of us is often unsustainable, unmanageable, and not conducive to effective teaching.	To focus on things that matter most and to improve wellbeing, we should reduce, not just manage, workload.
Reducing workload – Notes for leaders	

Part 5. Ensuring success

In the final section, success is our focus. What does it mean to different teachers at different stages of their careers? This section will unpack different routes to success in teaching.

Problem	Solution
Chapter 11 In teaching, there are many competing definitions of success.	Define what success means for you (but don't hold the definition too tightly).
Ensuring success – Notes for leaders	

Who Faces These Challenges?

Of course, all teachers face these challenges to a greater and lesser degree. Any teacher might face the challenges outlined above, and we'll all know colleagues who are struggling with them. In writing this book, I have two types of teachers in mind.

Firstly, the teacher who wants the job to be sustainable for the long term

I was talking to a school leader recently about how he was trying to help a new teacher at his school. The school leader explained that the new teacher was complaining about working until 6:30 every night and still has more to do. Sighing, the school leader remarked that the new teacher would just have to get used to it. Really? This inexperienced colleague was struggling and unhappy but that's just what they have to expect?

The Organisation for Economic Co-operation and Development (OECD) surveys teachers to better understand working conditions around the world. In 2018, the survey found that secondary teachers in England work, on average, 46.9 hours per week. Of course, such numbers mask variation within the teaching profession and across phases. A survey conducted in February 2022 by Teacher Tapp found that 45% of primary teachers and 38% of secondary teachers reported working over 50 hours in the previous week. A large chunk of teachers are regularly working more than ten-hour days, five days a week.

It is likely not possible to answer the question, *How many hours does a teacher need to work to be effective?* How would we measure this? How would we isolate the working hours from other factors? But we can start to think about how many hours teachers *think* they need to work to be successful. Most teachers say they can't complete the jobs they need to in their contracted hours.[3] Only 39% of primary teachers and 49% of secondary teachers believe it is possible to do the job well on less than 45 hours a week.[4] And, if that's what teachers think, we can bet that this affects our feelings of success. Unfortunately, further data from Teacher Tapp suggests that wellbeing suffers considerably once weekly hours creep above 50.[5] There must be another way.

Teachers tend to join the profession because they think they'll enjoy or be good at it.[6] Many remain in the profession because both turn out to be true. In writing this book, I want to help you get the obstacles and distractions out of the way so that you can enjoy being a good teacher.

Secondly, leaders who want the best for their staff

In a researchED talk, Dylan Wiliam describes the 'love the one you're with' strategy for staff development.[7] It's too easy for leaders to wish for different teachers. Or to be glad to see a teacher leave who had 'lost the love', without stopping to question what prompted that teacher to lose it in the first place, without stopping to assess what leaders could have done differently. Instead, leaders can 'love the one they're with' by focusing on the development of the teachers in front of them, by listening to those teachers, and by making every effort to help them sustain their careers in teaching.

At times, leaders get a poor deal, being made the scapegoat of problems beyond their control. Leaders are privileged, however, to work with more freedom than many of their colleagues. Having fewer classes and no tutor group in secondary schools means you can work differently than teachers with full timetables (even if your day is exceptionally busy in other ways).

If you're a leader, I hope that the advice in each section helps you grapple with the challenges you are facing. More than that, I hope the notes for leaders at the end of each section allow you to reflect honestly on the responsibility you hold, the power you have and how you wield it. This book is not down on school leaders, but, as a school leader, you have a responsibility not just to solve the problems that you face. You have a responsibility to support teachers you lead to cultivate sustainable careers.

It's rare that something so challenging and complex can be made easy in a moment. I'm not promising that. At the start of this book, all I ask is that you remain open-minded to the possibility that change could be made, that another approach might bring with it benefits or marginal improvements, and, ultimately, that the sum of these things could be a more enjoyable, sustainable career in teaching.

Notes

1 Kennedy, M. (2016). Parsing the practice of teaching. *Journal of Teacher Education*, 67(1), 6–17.
2 UCL News. Teachers' work intensity has risen to 'unprecedented' levels. (2021). Accessed from https://www.ucl.ac.uk/news/2021/jan/teachers-work-intensity-has-risen-unprecedented-levels (accessed on 4/12/2022).
3 Walker, M., Worth, J., and Van den Brande, J. (2019). *Teacher Workload Survey*. Department for Education. Accessed from https://assets.publishing.service.gov.uk/government/uploads/system/uploads/attachment_data/file/855933/teacher_workload_survey_2019_main_report_amended.pdf (accessed on 4/12/2022).
4 TeacherTapp. (2022). How many hours MUST teachers work for education to be excellent? (This, and other findings...). Accessed from https://teachertapp.co.uk/how-many-hours-must-teachers-work-for-education-to-be-excellent-this-and-other-findings/ (accessed on 18/11/2022).
5 TeacherTapp. (2023). What would make you stay in teaching? Accessed from https://teachertapp.co.uk/articles/what-would-make-you-stay-in-teaching/#:~:text=We%20can%20clearly%20see%20that,about%20burnout%2C%20stress%20and%20contentment (accessed on 3/1/2024).
6 Menzies, L., Parameshwaran, M., Shaw, B., and Chiong, C. (2015). *Why Teach?* Pearson. Accessed from: https://cfey.org/wp-content/uploads/2021/10/Why-Teach-1.pdf (Accessed on 10/9/24).
7 Wiliam, D. (2020). Teacher quality-what it is; why it matters; how to get more of it? ResearchEd Durrington Talk. Accessed from https://www.youtube.com/watch?v=BacHtPrh-qQ (accessed on 1/2/2023).

The Long Game

A school and the teachers and leaders in it saved my career in teaching. In 2012, my wife's job moved us from Bristol to Taunton, from a school just north of the city to a school in the town of Bridgwater. In Bristol, as an English teacher, I'd taught a travel writing scheme of work to Year 9. In one memorable sequence of lessons, we used an extract from a book called *Crap Towns: The 50 Worst Places to Live in the UK* [by Sam Jordison and Dan Kieran] which featured, and eviscerated, Bridgwater. How my colleagues and friends laughed when I told them I'd be heading to one of the 'crap towns.'

Maybe as a symptom of potential difficulties in our catchment, there was a much more intentional and supportive approach to behaviour. The headteacher sat down with me and talked through my most difficult classes and children and what I could do about them, what I could try. In my first week, he came to see me in my classroom and told me he'd heard great things about my lessons from the children. Later, he came into a lesson I was teaching and told the class they didn't know how lucky they were to have me as their teacher. He probably did this in every room, but it meant a lot to me. There was a clear system for managing behaviour. We didn't hide chaotic classrooms behind closed doors. Leaders were in lessons, to help not to check.

This, then, became the school where I made teaching work for me. The *Requires Improvement* school in Somerset was a more rewarding place to work than the *Good* one in the city. Unnecessary activity had been cut. Leaders had realistic expectations of teachers. Behaviour was not easy, but we were supported with it. I still look back with fondness to certain classes and colleagues. And I'm thankful for my experience at that school. It's not that everything was perfect from then on, but I found a rhythm I could sustain.

When I say a school, and its staff, saved my career in teaching, I don't mean that I did nothing and just let that happen. But I do mean it quite genuinely. I went from looking for jobs outside of teaching to loving coming to work.

Working at that school gave me an outlook that helped me in every subsequent job. An outlook focused on how to work effectively and productively in challenging

DOI: 10.4324/9781003453154-2

circumstances. An outlook I learned from great teachers and leaders, focused on what would maximise learning for all and what could be cut without losing anything. When I moved on to other schools and other roles, I took with me the experience of *a way* that worked, a way that helped me to find the joy in teaching.

The Pull to Conform

In the previous chapter, we introduced the persistent challenges of *being a teacher*:

- Sustaining motivation
- Managing intensity
- Embedding habits
- Reducing workload
- Ensuring success

Before we get to those challenges and potential solutions, we should consider why it can be difficult to address the specific challenges we face in and around the classroom.

Whenever a new idea is suggested for your classroom or your school, it makes sense to ask *What problem is this trying to solve?* Defining challenges before deciding solutions feels logical. *Surely everyone works in this way?* Too often, though, what we do as teachers is the accumulation of practice enforced by leaders and schools or encouraged by, implicitly or explicitly, our peers.

An experiment from the '50s sheds light on one of the core problems we're facing. Solomon Asch wanted to investigate the conditions in which individuals would submit to 'group pressure'.[1] A group was required – quite simply – to match a line with the closest in length from one of three different lines. They had to declare their judgements, their matches, publicly, but the task itself wasn't difficult. Usually, the answer was clear from a cursory glance at the different lines.

But, of course, there was a twist.

In the group of eight subjects, only one was really being examined. Seven of the group were planted to confidently assert the wrong answer. The eighth subject was left in 'possibly for the first time in his life, a situation in which a group unanimously contradicted the evidence of his senses.' You can imagine the raw anxiety of knowing something to be true – this line is like that one – but having seven other people say something else entirely. *Am I wrong? Am I seeing it wrong? Do I understand the task? What's happening?*

What was the result? In the control groups, where every member of the group completed the task properly, there were almost no errors in judgement. In the test groups, there was 'a marked movement toward the majority.' Not everyone changed their answer. Not everyone got every question wrong. But the pressure to conform was clear.

The experiment highlights what has come to be known as *conformity bias*, the adaptation of behaviour in response to implicit or explicit group pressure. Such a bias can work in positive and negative ways. If you work in a school where staff and leaders don't care about when teachers leave at the end of the day, there will be a healthy culture of going home when you need or want to. If you work in a school where everyone stays until 5:30 no matter what and leaving before then is frowned upon, it will be harder to pull away from conforming.

Here's the paradox and the problem of teaching: we feel the pull to conform to what we see in others, to the culture and the identity of *being a teacher*, but, if we want to succeed, we're going to have to break that mould. We're going to have to recognise how we're being pulled in directions that may be unhelpful or unproductive.

Difficult decisions are made to pull against a current which says *everything is essential, teachers must be busy*, or *teaching will always be this intense, this hard*, against an identity of the teacher which can be unhelpful. At times, this is straightforward. No one's told us we have to mark every page of every book. We've just convinced ourselves it's necessary. We grant ourselves permission not to mark excessively and go home a bit earlier. No one cares because no one expected it from us. We expected it from ourselves.

At times, finding a different, better approach is much, much harder. Leaders have mandated a practice where if you give a certain sanction, you have to call home. It's no longer a simple case of *giving yourself permission*. You can easily reach the end of a busy teaching day with ten phone calls to make. Ten phone calls on top of assessments and planning and feedback and life? What options does a teacher in this situation have? We'll look in greater depth at this sort of problem as we examine the challenges of being a teacher. But, even in these situations, we can find a way that teaching can work for us individually.

The Vocation Problem

The pull to conform isn't simply about practices or strategies that teachers use. We conform to the ideal of the teacher. To many, it would be bizarre to view teaching as anything other than a vocation. But vocation, a strong sense that you are suited for a particular role, is both an asset and a hindrance. Vocation is an asset because teaching is challenging. The hours can be long and the work is hard. Not only that, teaching offers emotional challenges which are probably rare outside of public service. Vocation then can drive us forward through these difficulties. Vocation offers a sense of mission and purpose that, at its best, can overcome the negativity.

Vocation is also a hindrance because it pushes us towards an approach to work that can be unhealthy: long hours and emotional investment which, for many, verge on a personal identity that is inextricably linked to being a teacher. Perhaps unsurprisingly, then, vocation is a facet of the problems we are trying to solve. At times as a positive force; at others, a negative one. We could summarise this contrast as follows:

Vocation is a positive force when...	Vocation is a negative force when...
• It motivates us to work hard and tackle the problems we're facing in the classroom. • It gives us a sense of purpose and mission when we turn up to work. • It helps us cope with and enjoy the intensity of the job.	• It prompts us to work harder than is sustainable or healthy. • It ties our identity to teaching in a way that makes receiving and responding to feedback difficult. • It makes it harder to switch off from teaching at the end of the day (or at weekends or on holidays).

As we examine the challenges teachers face through this book, it might be useful to consider when it is worth dialling up or down your sense of vocation. A tricky period with a class might prompt a dialling up of that sense of purpose in teaching as your chosen profession. Doing this helps us to focus on why you're a teacher even when things get tough. Dialling down that sense of vocation might be involuntarily prompted by changes in our lives. Returning from maternity leave could affect how long you can (or want to) stay at school, for example.

What Solutions are Offered (and Why do they Often Fail)?

Even when we look directly at the problems that teachers face, we can still swing and miss. Teachers know it's an intense job. We know workload is often difficult and sometimes close to impossible to manage. As a time-poor teacher, I recognise you come to this book looking for solutions, not platitudes or shallow tips and tricks. It's worth dwelling, then, on what won't be emphasised and what we'll avoid.

Work smarter

I once heard a headteacher tell his staff that if they just 'worked smarter' they would be out of the door earlier and enjoy teaching more. Bizarrely, this headteacher spoke as a detached observer rather than one of the instrumental drivers of workload. If teachers would just follow his advice, maybe they'd enjoy working in his school a bit more. Of course, they still had to do everything else he asked them to do.

Working smarter is often possible. It might help but it's probably not sufficient. Lots of the advice in this book might count as working smarter. But, too often, working smarter is a vague gesture towards superficial action. Is it working smarter to share resources as a department or phase team? Sure, but if those resources are poorly organised or incomplete, workload might increase by using them instead of decrease. If that school has complex or unusable systems, saving a little time elsewhere isn't going to help.

Wellbeing

I like to think that if someone tried to make me attend a yoga wellbeing session, I'd have resoluteness of character to *just say no*. If I'm honest, I'm probably too polite. I'd just do it to avoid upsetting anyone. Wellbeing sessions, staff yoga or netball, Cake Fridays – none of these is a bad thing, but they *generally* aren't solutions to the challenges mentioned above.

Schools and leaders should care about staff wellbeing. That much should be obvious, but what caring leads to is often less clear. Equally, if teachers want to look after their own wellbeing, what avenues can they pursue? You won't find suggestions here to manage wellbeing by eating cake and doing yoga (at least not at the same time).

How will this Book Differ?

Instead of simply rehashing these solutions, this book will take a different path. We will face the problems already mentioned head on. We will look at the possible solutions and consider honestly which problems such solutions might actually solve. My deeply held desire is that you can use this book to identify and address those areas that will make your teaching life more manageable, more enjoyable, and more sustainable.

Three principles make this book's approach to tackling the challenges of teaching distinct:

● **Pulling against conformity** – Hacks, tips, and tricks often paper over our problems. I won't try to repackage what you already know. We'll examine ways you could work differently to break down the challenges you're facing. We'll meet real teachers who have made teaching work for them.

● **A sustainable approach** – My aim is to offer strategies and solutions which will have impact over time and are manageable over time. Often, this is about more than introducing a new idea or two. It's about something much harder: changing our mind or our perspective on what it means to be an effective teacher.

● **Discerning challenges before deciding solutions** – If I tell you to try *Idea X*, all you can do is try it or not. *Idea X* might have an impact; it might not. It doesn't necessarily help you to solve future problems. Here, we're developing a perspective, not just implementing ideas. With sustainability and longevity as our aims, we can afford not to latch onto every new idea that comes our way. Examining the challenges of being a teacher means we can consider both which challenges are most pertinent to us *and* whether an approach we've thought of or heard about will really help us to meet those challenges.

Key Takeaways

- Identifying the specific problems before deciding on solutions might seem obvious, but schools and teachers often jump to solutions and strategies before truly defining the problem.

- Conformity bias is our tendency to align our beliefs and actions with the group we're in. This can make it hard to break out of perceived norms even when breaking out is what we need to do to make teaching more sustainable and manageable. If you work with colleagues who all use a certain resource or strategy, you're likely to use it, too. If you work with colleagues who never pause at lunchtime, you're unlikely to take a break, either.

- A sense of vocation is a belief that you are particularly suited to a role or job. Many teachers rightly have a sense of vocation.

- Vocation can be positive when it helps us to deal with the challenges of the job – the hard work and long hours. Vocation can be detrimental when it causes overwork or allows us to put up with too much, particularly in areas like behaviour and workload.

- Solutions are often offered to teachers to solve the problems. One solution is to *Work smarter*. Tips, tricks, and hacks are offered to save time. This advice can be useful, but often it papers over broader problems.

- Some of the advice in this book could be seen as *Work smarter* advice, but I am not expecting you, in reading this book, to implement every aspect of it. Instead, you should be identifying problems and defining solutions.

- Teacher wellbeing is important. Schools that are able to offer optional wellbeing activities (like yoga or Couch to 5k) are supporting the wellbeing of their staff. However, leaders should focus on solutions to the challenges that teachers face, not just nice extras.

Note

1 Asch, S. (1951). Effects of group pressure on the modification and distortion of judgements. In Guetzkow, H. (Ed.), *Groups, Leadership and Men*. Pittsburgh: Carnegie Press.

PART I
Sustaining Motivation

Problems	Solutions
Chapter 2  Lack of autonomy increases stress levels and negatively impacts wellbeing.	Maximise feelings of control and push back against autonomy-sapping practices.
Chapter 3 Teaching is an isolating profession.	Become an even more effective team member.
Chapter 4 When our development stalls, so does our motivation.	Commit to sustainable improvement.

DOI: 10.4324/9781003453154-3

2 Autonomy

Problem Lack of autonomy increases stress levels and negatively impacts wellbeing.	**Solution** Maximise feelings of control and push back against autonomy-sapping practices.

Zoe has been teaching for nearly 30 years. In that time, she has been a class teacher, middle leader, and senior leader. She has taught in primary and middle schools in both the state and private sectors. She has taught every year group from reception through to Year 8. And, yes, she's done some supply too. Now, Zoe leads her phase, upper KS2.

As we start our conversation about what might sustain a successful career in teaching, she tells me, 'I'm living proof that if you change schools there's always a better school for you. Every school's different.' Whilst Zoe's worked in lots of schools she loves, including the one she works in now, she is keenly aware of the damaging practices that sap teacher autonomy. She describes sitting in staff meetings and being 'ridiculed because my planning didn't look like my colleagues" or the 'madness' of having her marking mocked because, as a leftie, it looked different from other people's.

In some ways, Zoe has spent her career seeking out autonomy where she could find it. Being told what to do isn't enough; Zoe needs to understand why. 'There's nothing worse than being told *You've got to do it this way because....*' That *because* becomes a pause, an absence of a clear reason or clear thinking for practices. She deliberately moved school when she found one where there was 'the freedom to adapt'. In making moves like this, Zoe has been conscious that 'when it's been absolutely awful' in a school, 'there's always a new challenge.'

DOI: 10.4324/9781003453154-4

Problem

Walking across the Downs at Nottingham Uni, I remember a kindling desire to *do something*, something useful and meaningful. I had already volunteered on summer youth camps and been going into a primary school to listen to readers. University English felt too grand for me; I wanted to be back in the classroom or at least the kind of classroom where I had enjoyed myself. I entered training brimming with quiet passion and purpose.

Within a couple of years, I'd want to quit.

I know my story is not unique. Teaching should, we can often feel, be its own motivator. The job is full of intrinsic rewards, joyful moments, and regular signs we're making progress. Yet teachers can still feel demotivated about turning up and teaching their classes. Often, this is about leadership practices: an impassable jungle of admin or apparently pointless jobs make the journey to those enjoyable, satisfying moments too difficult.

Sometimes, it's about our attitude to our work. The intensity of teaching can lead us to long for the holidays and wish away the moment. Of course, you're entitled to do that, but is this how we want to view the career we devote so much time to? One historian of work put it like this:

> Work is about a search for daily meaning as well as daily bread, for recognition as well as cash, for astonishment rather than torpor; in short, for a sort of life rather than a Monday through Friday sort of dying.[1]

There are, of course, good days and bad; there are struggles and lows. I won't discount them here, but one of the persistent challenges of being a teacher is to work your way through those things or to work to minimise the effect of them so you can get to and dwell in the good stuff. Your job is to aggressively beat back those practices, policies, and attitudes that steal the joy from teaching. The point of this chapter is not to turn you into a happy automaton but to make us consider how we can self-motivate in the face of all that might try to stop us.

Teachers begin careers with clear motivators to teach

In the office of the first English department I worked in, there was a sign leaning against the wall. It had been given to a member of the team on their birthday as a joke and, whilst mildly amusing, was not something they wanted to take home. At the top, it read 'Why teach?' At the bottom, 'July and August.'

Teachers do, in part, stay in the profession because of the structure of the job.[2] The length of the school day and long holidays aren't the main reasons that teachers get into teaching, however. Teachers tend to be more motivated by altruistic reasons – the desire to make a difference – as well as, quite often, the passion they have for a particular subject.[3]

The problem of teacher motivation is the gap between what has driven you to teach in the past and what gets in the way of that now. It would not be unreasonable to suggest that your motivation is not always something completely in your control. *I'm motivated to teach but not to fill in spreadsheets....* How we motivate when so much feels out of our control then becomes incredibly important.

Quantity and types of work can demotivate

Mark is a mid-career, second in science. Too often, the sheer quantity and types of work descend around him like a fog, obscuring the joys of the job. When the fog lifts, he remembers the love he has for nurturing curiosity and knowledge.

Each morning, shortly after 7, Mark walks into his lab with some sense of promise. He's excited about his role, in particular supporting the new teachers and developing the Science curriculum. Tasks pile up quickly: parents to call, lessons to plan, books to mark, data to enter. It isn't only the pile that worries him. A heavy feeling that these jobs don't matter weighs on much of his day. He doesn't care about data entry and, as a good scientist, is concerned about the validity of the data. He knows feedback can help students but isn't sure the school's policy for marking is helping anyone.

The rapid accumulation of low-value tasks saps his motivation for the bits of the job he does enjoy. Getting to the end of the day, Mark no longer has the energy or the drive to engage in the deep thinking, the important work, he hoped his day would contain.

When we perceive that a task is going to stretch or exceed the limits of our mental capacity, we're less likely to engage with it.[4] So all of those challenging things we know we *need to get to* are harder to start because our mind is telling us that we'll have difficulty completing them. How often does something stay on your to-do list because it's not clear how to start it or because, after a five-period day, you don't feel like you have the mental energy for it?

Equally, perceived value massively affects our motivation. Where a task doesn't seem inherently interesting or rewarding or where it doesn't feel useful, motivation suffers.[5] We're all too aware of this feeling. We're keen for our students to make progress, but time must be given to arcane marking or data-entry practices. We want to promote positive behaviours in our classroom, but the behaviour policy reads like a mortgage application. We want to plan engaging and content-driven lessons, but a requirement to evidence certain behaviours or fit the school logo onto every slide drowns out our enjoyment.

When we expect to do low-value work, when we expect to be overloaded, our ability to self-motivate is diminished. Even when we expect high-value tasks, if we don't have the cognitive capacity, the headspace, to manage those tasks, we're likely to make slow progress with them or even disengage.

Self-determination theory

Mark's sense of disconnect between that desire to teach and the reality of teaching is partly the cumulative effect of each overloaded day. A quantity of thinking and tasks that strains his capacity to focus or consider all that he must retain, consider, and do.

If he had to describe it, he'd put it like this: *It's easier to maintain what I'm doing – plan lessons, emails, the odd call to a parent – rather than change it. I know I'd like it more if I was working with the team. I know I'd like to think about the subject more than I do when I'm planning and marking and in meetings. But it's hard to get from here to there. It's easier in the routine.* Mark doesn't feel in control.

The problem is that teaching, which should be so satisfying, can leave us unsatisfied. Why is this? To understand, we need to delve into human motivation. Richard Ryan and Edward Deci, the originators of Self-Determination Theory (SDT), offer us a way we can view and understand what motivates and demotivates us. Humans are motivated by, if not the same, then similar things. SDT defines the needs that motivate human actions, those things we see as essential for ongoing satisfaction in our lives.

To start with, Ryan and Deci remind us why motivation is important. Because 'motivation produces.'[6] When we're motivated, we get results. All the more important for us, then, to see motivation as something we manage and are in control over rather than as a reserve sapped by forces beyond our control.

SDT states that there are three core 'universal psychological needs' that, when met, promote intrinsic motivation, internalised motivation rather than a need for external rewards.[7] The three needs are

- Autonomy – The sense that we have control over our behaviour and decisions.

- Relatedness – The need for 'close and secure'[8] relationships with others.

- Mastery – The 'need to be effective'[9] in our life at work and beyond.

The satisfaction of these needs during an activity has been linked to better engagement in that activity. The reverse is also true, however: where these needs are not met or even diminished, motivation is sapped. Let's look at these needs in relation to teaching.

The three chapters in this section of the book take each of Ryan and Deci's needs and look at them with a focus on how schools and teachers meet them and what goes wrong when we don't. For now, we'll focus on autonomy.

Non-negotiable

Some schools list their 'non-negotiables': classroom practices or general behaviours that *everyone* must follow. On the face of it, this feels sensible. We achieve more when we row together. In a school where behaviour or high level of need poses a particular problem, ensuring all staff use the same language makes sense.

Where the defined behaviours are few, with clear reasons for each, they can be a positive force in a school.

However, the language of the 'non-negotiable' can do more harm than good. Even where teachers are autonomous in all sorts of areas, the language itself saps the intellectual life from teaching and, importantly, the feeling that we are autonomous. In a graduate profession, with committed staff-bodies, it is bizarre to over-dictate or underestimate the abilities of teachers.

I once sat in a meeting where over 20 non-negotiables were introduced in a particularly dire September Inset (in-service training). Staff began to raise their hands and offer exceptions, problems and alternatives to what was probably a list hastily cobbled together. Before our eyes, these non-negotiables were negotiated.

Degrees of autonomy

Teachers who have autonomy feel more effective and experience higher levels of wellbeing.[10] Even in areas where an increase in autonomy may lead to an increase in workload, there still seem to be positive effects of autonomy: teachers who had high levels of control over the curriculum they taught experienced less stress than those with less control.[11]

Autonomy is clearly a *good thing*. But, and there has to be a *but*, the quantity and quality of that autonomy, the shape that it should take, are by no means clear. Total freedom and total control are illusory at best. The headteacher isn't totally free to act in any way they want. Equally, wanting to be left alone isn't a realistic ambition in any organisation. We don't need or want to create a unique behaviour policy in every classroom, and autonomy is not the same as a say in every leadership decision made in the school. Organisations share practices to meet shared goals effectively and efficiently. Not every constraint on autonomy points to an excess of dictatorial leadership.

The problem of autonomy, then, is not simply that we should have more of it. The right kind of autonomy could be a strong motivator, but understanding what we could or should expect in this area is less straightforward.

Perhaps it's useful to see ideal teacher autonomy as two sides of the same coin:

- A negative side, the areas where our autonomy shouldn't be curtailed.

- A positive side, the spaces where we should have freedom to act in a way that seems best to us.

We might express these sides of the coin like this:

- *I should be able to decide not to do X.*

- *I want the freedom to do Y.*

Rather than having a definitive list of practices we could place on both sides, the sides give us ways of thinking about and evaluating our autonomy.

Solutions

Mark, our second in Science, decided to book in the activities that he sees as important, the things most deeply connected to what drove him to teach. He realises that he might need to work differently. He might need to be honest about some of the jobs he is expected to do.

Mark made sure his week includes some time set aside to specifically delve into subject knowledge related to the following week's lessons. No one needed to give him permission to do this. He just decided to. It's now a regular feature on his calendar, a time he looks forward to. At times, he reads a relevant article; at others, he scripts an explanation or plans a practical.

Mark also reluctantly and nervously gave some feedback on the feedback policy. He explained his concerns graciously and precisely. The Assistant Head listened and then did something surprising. As long as Mark follows the principles of the policy, he can adapt it to suit his needs.

These changes are relatively small wins, but they have reminded Mark that he has some control over the way he works. Not total control but some. That has been enough to remind him that there is a lot he enjoys about being a teacher.

Remember your personal motivators

Before we get to specific solutions for a lack of autonomy, let's consider what motivated you to become a teacher. Research suggests it's likely that this was a desire to make a difference, to share a love of subject, or to work with young people. One way to recapture that drive to teach is to plan one activity each day that takes you back to what motivated you to teach to begin with. This doesn't have to be a big, time-consuming thing. Instead, it's the little acts, the daily reminders of what teaching can and should be.

If subject is your passion, setting aside extra time tomorrow to delve a little further than normal planning allows into a subject area you're interested in might help. If you love those conversations with young people but feel you're missing out stuck in your classroom, intentionally go and start one conversation with someone on duty. Small acts can be equally impactful. As you write the title on the board, remind yourself what you love about this topic. As a student asks a question bound to send you down a tangential rabbit hole, use it as a reminder of how much you used to love and nurture curiosity.

Such acts are personal to us. The way you trigger these feelings will be different from the colleague next door. Less about forcing ourselves to be happy at each moment of the day, this is about you keenly focusing – at least once a day – on what has tied you personally to teaching.

Be clear on the autonomy that matters to you

Instead of wanting *more freedom* or *to be left to do my job*, consider what you want more freedom *from* or *to do*. Is it in the planning and creation of lesson resources? Is it the style, the strategies, and the techniques of teaching in your classroom? Is it how you spend your time?

Define what types of freedom you value in teaching. Set aside a short time to think about this. Don't seek out more freedom for its own sake. Push further into those areas where freedom would bring you greater joy, greater fulfilment, greater wellbeing.

If every day you feel got at, controlled, and dictated to, it might be worth considering why, particularly when others don't feel the same. I once worked in a school where I felt utterly out of sync with the way of doing things. I left every meeting bursting with further reasons to be frustrated. I didn't like the way behaviour was managed, homework was run, leadership was done. These areas and others felt like they were constraining my autonomy largely because I knew I'd do things differently if I could. I was out of sync not just with the school but with my colleagues, many of whom shared my frustrations but never to the degree that I held them. They had worked at the school for years, and many continue there quite happily.

For a while, I tried to 'fix' what was in my power to fix, to influence where I could influence. But creating a school in your image or bending it to your ideals is unlikely to work. Realising this is what we're trying to do, we have a couple of options:

- **Accept** – At times, it may be possible to say *This is where I am right now. I don't like lots of it, but I don't have to fight against it.* Life will offer plenty of reasons why we can't just leave the job we're finding difficult. We might use the mantra *This is temporary* to remind ourselves that we're not accepting limits on our autonomy.

- **Leave** – I did my best to leave that school but not at the expense of transplanting my frustrations to another school. I went into application processes and interview days aware of how miserable I'd been.

Evaluate your autonomy

Assess, for a moment, the autonomy you feel you have over everyday activities. Two exercises could help you define how much control you have over those activities:

a. **Make two lists**. First, list what you have control over. This might be how you teach or give feedback, how you make contact with home or do your planning. Second, list those things you don't feel control over, those areas that may be dictated. If it isn't easy to make these lists distinct and separate, you could do the same thing but with a spectrum from 'Total control' to 'No control.'

b. **Evaluate your lists**. I've often spoken to teacher friends working in other schools and been amazed by how much can be dictated to teachers. Whilst commiserating with them, I've recognised that, for much of my career, I've had more control than many other teachers over planning, teaching style, and so on. Evaluate the lists you've made. Are they what you expected? What are you thankful to be in control of? Where you lack the power to choose, what particularly frustrates you?

c. **Act, feedback, or leave it**. For every item that frustrates you, you have three options. Perhaps we can *act* to change how we feel about an item. We realise there is scope to take more control of a particular area. For example, a feedback policy might promote an approach but offer scope for choice where staff want it. Or we're allowed to adapt resources or content for certain topics but don't feel we have the time. Acting isn't easy. It requires a change to our behaviour (something we'll talk more about in Chapters 7 and 8), but if it's possible, it might help us to feel more autonomous. If frustration is creeping towards resentment because we genuinely aren't in control of a certain area, it's worth giving feedback to leaders. Finally, we might decide that we don't want to commit the effort or don't mind that we lack autonomy in certain areas. We *leave* that area alone, at least for now.

Return after Chapters 3 and 4

Isolating our potential needs into chapters in this book hopefully helps us to reflect on them individually. However, care should be taken to avoid seeing them in total isolation. The next two chapters deal with relatedness and mastery. These needs can interact with and supersede autonomy, depending on how important they are to us.

A professional development programme might severely limit autonomy – we're told what to do, we practise that thing and receive feedback on it – but we enjoy the feeling of mastery that comes with it. Motivation doesn't dip. Or shared planning limits the choices we make about what to teach and how, but the sense of working together towards a shared goal remains a powerful motivator. We'll look more on these motivators in the next two chapters.

If you're concerned about motivation but autonomy doesn't feel like the right place to look right now, move onto the next two chapters and return to consider autonomy in light of the other needs.

Key Takeaways

● Teachers join the profession for largely altruistic reasons as well as, particularly in secondary, a passion for a subject. Teachers do stay in teaching for some practical reasons, like holidays.

- Perceived value of a task affects our motivation to complete it. When we accumulate perceived low-value tasks, we can struggle to motivate ourselves to work through them.

- Self-Determination Theory posits that humans have three needs that must be met – and continue to be met – in order to feel motivation. These three needs are autonomy, relatedness, and mastery.

- Autonomy correlates with higher wellbeing and lower stress levels. Schools and leaders might rightly enforce certain common behaviours that solve the problems the school is facing. However, this should be done with care because they endanger teacher motivation.

- Teachers can decide what sort of autonomy and how autonomy is important to them. We can also audit the autonomy. Acceptance of autonomy-sapping practice is possible. As is deciding which practices to question and critique and which to concede.

- At times, as Zoe suggested at the start, we might decide that leaving is our best option, but this is decision not to be taken lightly.

Notes

1 Terkel, S. (1974). *Working: People Talk about What They Do All Day and How They Feel about What They Do.* London: New Press.
2 Menzies, L., Parameshwaran, M., Trethewey, A., Shaw, B., Baars, S., and Chiong, C. (2015). *Why Teach?* LKMco report.
3 Menzies, L., Parameshwaran, M., Trethewey, A., Shaw, B., Baars, S., Chiong, C. *Why Teach?*
4 Feldon, D., Callan, G., Juth, S., and Jeong, S. (2019). Cognitive load as motivational cost. *Educational Psychology Review.* Review article. *31*(2), 319–337.
5 Feldon, D., Callan, G., Juth, S., and Jeong, S. Cognitive load as motivational cost.
6 Ryan, R., and Deci, E. (2000). Self-determination theory and facilitation of intrinsic motivation, social development and wellbeing. *American Psychologist*, 55(1), 68–78.
7 Jang, H., Reeve, H. Ryan, R., and Kim, A. (2009). Can self-determination theory explain what underlies the productive, satisfying learning experiences of collectivistically oriented Korean students? *Journal of Educational Psychology*, 101(3), 644–661.
8 Jang, H., Reeve, H. Ryan, R., and Kim, A. Can self-determination theory explain what underlies the productive, satisfying learning experiences of collectivistically oriented Korean students?
9 Jang, H., Reeve, H. Ryan, R., and Kim, A. Can self-determination theory explain what underlies the productive, satisfying learning experiences of collectivistically oriented Korean students?
10 Yukselir, C., and Ozer, O. (2022). Investigating the interplay between English language teachers' autonomy, well-being and efficacy. *Issues in Educational Research*, 32(4), 1643–1657.
11 Pearson, L., and Moomaw, W. (2005). The relationship between teacher autonomy and stress, work satisfaction, empowerment, and professionalism. *Educational Research Quarterly*, 29(1), 38–54.

3 Relatedness

 Problem
Teaching is an isolating profession.

Solution
Become an even more effective
team member.

After 30 years in teaching, Zoe's been in too many teams to count. She currently works in a school with one of the more challenging catchments in the county. Yet the school has relatively low staff turnover. What does Zoe attribute this to? 'We work as a team.' For Zoe, 'Team is what makes you stay regardless of what type of school it is.' In contrast, Zoe has worked in schools where it's all about 'one-upmanship and everyone is competing.' In these schools, the lack of connection drains the life from teaching.

The best teams Zoe has worked in do three things. First, workload and, in particular, planning are shared. Second, there is openness and honesty; you can say *'I've had a bad day and I don't know how to deal with this* and be able to share it.' Third, connection with colleagues as people; you 'have a laugh' and 'know them as people.'

Problem

Some of the best moments in my career, the times I've really looked forward to, have been lunch times and break times in the staffroom or the workroom with colleagues. What, then, is the problem? We work with colleagues who can engage and encourage us, who make us laugh and commiserate through our failures. Surely this is a motivator? Of course, it is, but teaching can funnel us into isolation rather than making the most of these connections.

Let's consider how teaching can do that and why it's a problem and then examine some solutions.

DOI: 10.4324/9781003453154-5

In isolation

How many times have I got to the end of a lesson and thought, *I'm glad no one saw that*? The isolation of the teacher in the classroom, at least a lot of the time, has its benefits. Whilst lots of the job can be done *with others* – planning, for example – the act of teaching we do by ourselves. More than this, schools have become more compartmentalised. Silos have, at times almost literally, been built where staffrooms are demolished to make way for departmental or phase workrooms. Even where staffrooms do exist, staff often don't visit.[1]

How much is this a problem? You might be happy turning up, doing your job, and going home. You might experience connection in other ways within or beyond the school day. You might actually go to the staffroom. Relatedness is not simply about seeing and talking to other people during the average work day.

One set of researchers sums up relatedness as 'the need to experience mutual care and concern for close others.'[2] *Mutual*. Motivation is unlikely to stir from lots of excessively saccharine encounters each day. What matters is that you feel a sense of connection to those you work with. You could call this teamwork, community, a shared mission. Understanding relatedness like this makes it about more than just visiting the staffroom. It's the extent to which we're connected by a common purpose or goal as well as a common space we inhabit.

Friends at work

Common purpose doesn't have to be a cold, utilitarian contracting with colleagues. It seems we work better with friends, but only around a third of teachers say they have good friends or a best friend at work.[3] Whilst this might sound a little playground, the importance of friendship at work is an area of burgeoning research. People with a best friend at work are more likely to

- Have higher job satisfaction
- Get more done
- Share more ideas
- Have more fun[4]

Perhaps this feels obvious, but the culmination of these effects is the high likelihood[5] that those with a best friend will stay in their current job.

It's easy to see why. When TeacherTapp asked over 9000 teachers what affected their morale, they received over 60,000 words in response. After the answers of the teachers with the highest morale were analysed, two words stood out: *team* and *supportive*.[6] High morale, it seems, is driven by those connections forged with colleagues as we work towards a common goal.

Two valid but conflicting angles may be suggested by this finding. Firstly, we could mourn the absence of any kind of team or support. I'm not here to contradict your experience. If your morale is low, there may be insurmountable obstacles in your current school to reaching more optimistic, happier climes. Toxic workplaces do exist. By action or omission, school leaders, or colleagues, can create an environment where support is limp and team is a distant fantasy. My encouragement to find and give support or embrace your team when you're working in an environment like this is unhelpful at best.

But there is a second scenario, a second angle, that might find this and other research or insights useful. The nature of extremes means that most of us don't work in that toxic environment. Lots of us might work in an environment that could be better, could be more supportive, more connected. The solutions below offer ways to cultivate better connection, better teamwork, better support – to you *and* from you. How much ownership you can take of these things isn't entirely up to you. Our focus here is on what we *can* control.

Solutions

Mel is Head of English at an average-sized comprehensive school in Somerset. You might expect that, once you take on some kind of leadership role, a person could start to feel detached from their team. But not Mel. If anything, leading a group of English teachers has made her think more about what it means to work in an effective team. She explains, 'Though I'm head of department, I don't feel like I can't go to the team for support. It feels very collegiate.'

Mel's English department, like many teams in secondary schools, has a tiny workroom that barely fits them all at lunchtime. We talk in this workroom, and, as I sit down, I sort of yelp in surprise as I sink low into a chair, worn and weathered by many English teachers. The workroom is a place to relax and talk but also to 'bounce ideas off each other'. Mel explains, 'We'll talk about what we're teaching, how we taught it, things that worked and things that haven't. There's lots of incidental reflective practice, lots of support as well.'

A team helps in other ways. They genuinely work together so 'The upside of having a large team is that you still have the same amount of work to do in terms of preparation and resourcing but with the larger team there's more people to share that workload with.' Here, Mel is both pragmatic and reflective. The team help to save each other time, but they also act as a source of development so 'You've got more people to learn from.'

Relatedness in work relationships

An obvious answer to a feeling of lack when it comes to relatedness is to spend more time with colleagues. Just spending the time, though, won't help us to be effective and might diminish our ability to get things done and leave when we want to. We should, then, consider *how* we spend time with colleagues and *what* we spend that time for.

Happier people, evidence suggests, are more likely to help co-workers and devote time to relationships with them.[7] Are they happy because they do this? Or do they do this because they're happy? If we're willing to take a chance, it doesn't exactly matter. Instead of over-thinking it, we can act ourselves towards better connection, higher morale, and greater motivation to teach.

If our problem is isolation, our solution is to, literally and figuratively, walk out of our classroom down the corridor. Where planning has been a lone journey through unfamiliar territory, finding our way might be easier with someone alongside us. Where behaviour management has been a battle we're ill equipped for, a colleague at our back might be the support we need.

Of course, this might all sound a bit ridiculous to you. *I have friends. I'm connected to colleagues. I don't need you to tell me....* But remember the problem we're trying to solve. I'm not, and this chapter is not, here to help you make a couple of friends at work. Teaching is a naturally isolating profession. Symptoms of that isolation might include

- A feeling of being overwhelmed by the day-to-day tasks of the teacher

- A sense of drudgery that each day brings more of the same, another pile of work to get through alone

- A concern that colleagues are racing ahead with solutions to problems you're facing.

If those are problems we'd like to tackle, this chapter might be for you. Relatedness might offer a solution.

Relatedness also offers a solution to a wider problem. Researchers who conducted a decades-long study on happiness found that 'Relationships are not just essential as stepping-stones to other things, and they are not simply a functional route to health and happiness. They are ends in themselves.' Why? Because 'Positive relationships are essential to human well-being.'[8] Our relationships at work aren't just transactions, exchanging expertise and attention on each other's problems. Positive relationships are likely to reduce our stress, improve our health, and, ultimately, make us happy.[9] Whether the problems above relate specifically to us here and now, they are worth our time and attention.

There are several things we can do to build a sense of relatedness in what we do:

- Cultivate habits of friendship

- Be a better team member

- Join wider communities

Let's look at those in turn.

Cultivate habits of friendship

Every so often, you'll hear someone give the advice *make friends with the care-taker; they're a helpful person to be on the right side of*. As if friendly behaviour is solely for personal gain. Ulterior motives may exist for being friendly with colleagues, but if the motive is a better sense of human connection at work, I think we're alright.

To get to deeper, purposeful relatedness at work, let's examine two characteristics worth developing:

- Humility
- Vulnerability

Humility

The path between humility and false humility is a dangerous one to walk. No-one likes a colleague who bemoans their lack of ability in an area where they are clearly competent. In this way, humility is difficult to *get right*. You can't just go into work tomorrow and choose something to say you're bad at in an effort to connect with your colleagues. Before we look at *how* we might show humility, let's examine *why* it could be important.

When we express humility, we make it more likely that our colleagues around us feel safe to do the same. They probably feel more connected and closer to us as well.[10] We're likely to encounter more ideas, to learn more, to be challenged more when we're intellectually humble than when we think the answers – all of them – are simply and solely somewhere inside ourselves.[11]

Humility might be seen through discussion of recent successes, both ours and of those around us. We've all encountered a colleague who was so taken with their own successes that they talked of little else. Those colleagues will interrupt your discussion of recent challenges to share how well *they* are doing. They might even commit the cardinal sin of the teaching profession and tell you, 'Well, they behave for *me.*'

When we brag often, we're likely to come across as cold to our colleagues. But when we couple or balance that bragging with praise for what *others* have done, how *others* have handled situations, we're seen more favourably and are more likely to forge stronger connections with those colleagues.[12]

Vulnerability

Perhaps there's not much light between humility and vulnerability. We could do worse than see vulnerability as a facet of our humility. Out of humility comes vulnerability. Out of vulnerability comes a request for help, an admission of error, a call for support.

How willing are you to do those things? Let's focus on one. How willing are you to admit a mistake? Perhaps it depends on the mistake or whom you have to admit it to. When everyone around us seems to get so much right, admitting we've got something wrong can feel like a step too far. Research suggests that those of us who are hard on ourselves, who don't want to admit a mistake for fear of the reaction, are much harder on ourselves than those we worry about admitting the mistake to.[13] When we work ourselves up and worry about admitting we don't know something or have messed something up, the likeliest reaction is respect and acceptance, not judgement.

What can I do now?

- Reflect on your strengths and your weaknesses. Where could you ask for help? Or admit a mistake? Where might you be overestimating your abilities? It isn't always easy to ask these questions, but it's worth doing. Humility and vulnerability can't grow when strangled by a lack of self-awareness.

- Praise colleagues publicly for what you see them do well. When we're in the habit to do this, it is natural and free. When there isn't a culture of praise in our team or it doesn't come naturally, it can feel forced and awkward. Start small.

- Regularly ask *How do you...? How do you manage Year 3 after lunch? How are you introducing handball to Year 9? You've taught Finn before, haven't you? How have you supported him to stay in the room?* The act of asking the question is not the same as admitting weakness, but it does show deference to the wisdom of our peers. Asking lots of questions, and asking to truly learn, puts us in the stance of humility so that we're ready to do just that.

- Admit mistakes and admit we're lost. We don't have to manufacture a mistake to do this; we don't have to force ourselves to lose our way. Save this until we need it. A complaint from a parent has blindsided us. Behaviour that had once been manageable is now out of control. A topic we've taught for weeks has been totally misunderstood. Explaining this to a colleague can feel like a step too far, like we're revealing something sullied and shameful. Colleagues, though, are less likely to see it this way.

If we want to be genuine as we seek genuine connection and genuine support, we find ways to express our humility through our vulnerability. The gains are many and varied: deeper connection, deeper support, the wisdom of colleagues, learning and new ideas, the satisfaction of relatedness, a sense of our work *together*.

Be a better team member

Steve, who had a career in business before a career in teaching, points out that 'Teaching is a far more isolated' job than his roles in retail or finance ever were. Because of the nature of the classroom, being a teacher means that, for large portions of your day, 'you haven't got anyone to turn to.' Steve's point isn't that teamwork doesn't exist in schools but that it mainly 'exists outside of the classroom.' How we connect, work together, support each other, all this is so important because when we go into the classroom, we're generally on our own.

We've seen that being in a team, connected to others, is a source of morale and motivation. What, then, can or should we do to practically tap into the morale-boosting power of the team? Let's look at two things:

1. Foster connection through interdependence.

2. Become an agent of team cohesion.

Foster connection through interdependence

In a way, we've already started. Humility and vulnerability are essential. Better teachers seem to be quicker to go to their colleagues for advice. Better teachers, or at least those seen that way, are also sought for their advice.[14] In this way, they do two things innate to the good team member:

- Be dependable.

- Depend on others.

We are dependable when we do what we say we will but, more than that, we are ready to support and help, to advise and challenge.

Interdependence is tricky. If you like to be in control, agreeing with a colleague to share out the resourcing for upcoming lessons can induce anxiety. Approaching the days before the lessons when *their* resources are needed, you start to feel a nagging desire to ask them whether the resources are ready, when they'll be ready, what they'll contain.

Equally, being dependable means being open and ready to help. You're planning during planning, preparation, and assessment (PPA), and a colleague comes into your room. They've upset the teaching assistant who works with a boy in their class and want your take on their plan to make things right. It's easy to think, in that moment, *I don't want to help; I just want to do my work.*

Being dependable means getting organised. A request made by a colleague goes on your list or into your calendar so you know you won't forget it. Perhaps some colleagues are able to remember every conversation, every need and problem you've expressed. Perhaps those colleagues, through instinct or intuition, are able to turn up at the right moment with just the solution. The rest of us need to organise.

Become an agent of team cohesion

There's a problem with cohesion, isn't there? We don't choose our team. We're put in Year 4, or, as an English teacher, we find ourselves in the English team. Teammates are present when we arrive; a team culture exists. Whether we like each other feels like an accident of fate. My goal could be to be the best English teacher I can be, to get the best results for my students. Yours might be to get through the day.

Unsurprisingly, teams that cohere are more effective and efficient.[15] Time is saved. Such teams are full of people who like each other (at least a little), are committed to the same goals, and are proud of being part of the team.[16]

Two ways to be an agent of team cohesion:

● **See success as dependent on team cohesion**. A summary of research into teams suggests that team cohesion – in particular, strong work cohesion – can predict a team's success.[17] If we prioritise the team's success, we start to work differently. In some schools, teachers are very protective of their resources, sometimes to the point of not sharing them with colleagues or not leaving them for colleagues when they move to a new school. Others work entirely alone, happily shunning shared planning or other team activities. If we want team cohesion, if we want team success, we see value in contributing to that success by supporting those around us.

● **Be the person who includes all members of a team in a discussion**. Whether it's a meeting, a chat at lunchtime, or a debate about where to go for the Christmas meal, be the person who – unfailingly – asks to hear the voice of the colleague who isn't heard often enough.

Jane has been a teacher in the Year 3 team at her school for two years. When she joined the school, she was told that the three members of the team had PPA together to 'co-plan'. In reality, this means they sit silently in an office together during PPA time. Each member of the team has a planning responsibility – Jane has been focused on Maths – but this isn't something that is discussed in the shared time. Instead, one person makes the resources for a unit and drops them into the shared area and then colleagues have a cursory look through before teaching.

Jane is conscious that neither teachers nor children are getting a good deal. Sometimes, she opens resources planned by her colleagues and doesn't understand what they intended. She respects her colleagues: they're knowledgeable and experienced. But she knows the team could be getting so much more from each other.

Jane decides to do two things. Firstly, she expresses her humility and a little vulnerability by admitting that her class, and Jane herself , are struggling with the writing lessons at the moment. She doesn't critique the resources; she just asks the experienced colleague planning them to spend a bit of time talking through how they'd use the resources. She asks her head for a short amount of cover to observe this colleague teaching writing, which is agreed. During break, after this observation, Jane doesn't have to act when she praises her colleague's masterful teaching of the writing curriculum. Secondly, Jane offers to spend ten minutes at the end of the shared PPA time going through her Maths resources. One colleague takes her up on this, and it starts to become a semi-regular fixture.

Over time, Jane's team start to do more together rather than simply sharing workload and explaining their planning. She reflects that nothing has changed in terms of structures or systems – the team have always had PPA together – but the way they're using that time has changed dramatically.

Join wider communities

A drive to *be better*, to get better at teaching, drove me to research. I began reading whatever I could find. I'm not sure this made me a better teacher, not immediately at least. I understood vaguely what better teaching might look like, what it might include. In my own practice, I saw glimpses of it but fleeting ones.

With mild embarrassment, I admitted to my wife that I wanted to attend an educational conference in my spare time. That first conference I didn't know anyone, but there was a mad encouragement that came from being surrounded by over 1000 teachers who all wanted to talk about research on a Saturday.

There are professional groups and networks for specific subjects, PSHE (personal, social, health and economic education) leads, Early Years Leads, and lots of other roles. These groups provide resources, ideas, and training for teachers and leaders. But they also place us in a web of like-minded colleagues, colleagues facing the same challenges as us and striving towards the same measure of success. Connections like these humble us as we recognise that our approach is not unique; the reverse is also true: they open different routes to the same destination, other ways of reaching success that we had not yet considered.

What can you do now to join and connect with these networks? Three things:

- **Read**. Most networks release blogs or articles that elucidate the views and ideas of teachers within the network. If you go to the CogSciSci[18] webpage, you'll find a blog with reflections from a wide range of voices. The same is true of LitDrive and Maths Conf. It is not hyperbole to say that at no other time in the history of teaching have we had such access to the thoughts and ideas of like-minded (and not-so-like-minded) colleagues.

- **Conferences**. Each of the organisations mentioned above (and lots more) runs a semi-regular conference. Some are on Saturdays, some mid-week. Devoting a real chunk of time, investing a whole day, not just a spare moment to read a blog or two, in connecting with colleagues and their ideas forces you into a network in the way the other ideas here can't.

● **Engage**. I hesitate to mention social media as it can be a real drain on our time and a potential cause of an *always-on* mentality. We get home from work, having thought hard about work all day, and then read, discuss, and obsess over the ideas shared on platforms that were probably originally designed for us to connect with friends and family. That said, I'm not sure I'd be writing this book if I hadn't engaged in dialogue, mainly asking questions to start with, on Twitter with teachers who knew a lot more than me. Of course, social media is not the only way to engage in such dialogue. If you're at the in-person event, you can have those conversations face to face. Local networks for senior leaders or phase leaders can offer the opportunity to build, perhaps over time, strong connections with those in similar roles.

Key Takeaways

● Relatedness is driven by a 'mutual care and concern for others.' When we feel and experience it, motivation soars.

● Friendship at work is a powerful motivator with all manner of positive side effects. However, many teachers don't have strong friendships in their schools.

● Teacher morale is significantly affected by the teams we are in and the support we receive.

● Humility and vulnerability are particularly powerful traits to form meaningful friendships with colleagues. False humility and vulnerability do exist, but it's worth pushing towards the genuine by regularly praising others, admitting mistakes, and asking questions.

● Become an even better team member to nurture relatedness: foster interdependence and cohesion.

● Join networks within and beyond your school to connect with those solving similar problems, to learn from them, and to feel a sense of something bigger.

Notes

1 TeacherTapp. (2020). Will schools cope with a coronavirus closure? (Plus marker pens, staffroom sitting & other goodies). Accessed from https://teachertapp.co.uk/articles/will-schools-closr-cope-with-a-coronavirus-closure/ (accessed on 12/4/2022).

2 Vansteenkiste, M., Niemiec, C., and Soenens, B. (2010). The development of the five mini-theories of self-determination theory: An historical overview, emerging trends, and future directions. *The Decade Ahead: Theoretical Perspectives on Motivation and Achievement Advances in Motivation and Achievement*, 16A, 105–165.

3 TeacherTapp. (2023). Your friends at school, languages and the pandemic legacy. Accessed from https://teachertapp.co.uk/articles/your-friends-at-school-languages-and-the-pandemic-legacy/ (accessed on 17/8/2023).

4 Patel, A., and Plowman, S. (2023). The increasing importance of a best friend at work. *Gallup*. Accessed from https://www.gallup.com/workplace/397058/increasing-importance-best-friend-work.aspx (accessed on 17/8/2023).

5 There is a mixed picture on whether you're more likely to be happy at work if you have good friends. For example, TeacherTapp. (2023). Your friends at school, languages and the pandemic legacy. Accessed from https://teachertapp.co.uk/articles/your-friends-at-school-languages-and-the-pandemic-legacy/ (accessed on 17/8/2023).

6 TeacherTapp. (2023). Strikes, the key to morale, 'generating evidence', observations and pay. Accessed from https://teachertapp.co.uk/articles/strikes-the-key-to-morale-generating-evidence-observations-and-pay/ (accessed on 1/9/2023).

7 Lyubomirsky, S. (2008). *The How of Happiness: A Scientific Approach to Getting the Life You Want*. New York: Penguin Press.

8 Waldinger, R., and Schulz, M. (2023). *The Good Life*. London: Rider.

9 Waldinger, R., and Schulz, M. *The Good Life*.

10 Lehmann, M., Pery, S., Kluger, A. N., Hekman, D. R., Owens, B. P., and Malloy, T. E. (2023). Relationship-specific (dyadic) humility: How your humility predicts my psychological safety and performance. *Journal of Applied Psychology*, 108(5), 809–825.

11 Leary, M. R., Diebels, K. J., Davisson, E. K., Jongman-Sereno, K. P., Isherwood, J. C., Raimi, K. T., Deffler, S. A., and Hoyle, R. H. (2017). Cognitive and interpersonal features of intellectual humility. *Personality and Social Psychology Bulletin*, 43(6), 793–813.

12 VanEpps, E., Hart, E., and Schweitzer, M. E. (2022). Dual-promotion: Bragging better by promoting peers. George Mason University School of Business Research Paper. Available at SSRN: https://ssrn.com/abstract=4128132 or https://doi.org/10.2139/ssrn.4128132.

13 Bruk, A., Scholl, S. G., and Bless, H. (2022). You and I both: Self-compassion reduces self–other differences in evaluation of showing vulnerability. *Personality and Social Psychology Bulletin*, 48(7), 1054–1067.

14 Spillane, J. P., Shirrell, M., and Adhikari, S. (2018). Constructing "experts" among peers: Educational infrastructure, test data, and teachers' interactions about teaching. *Educational Evaluation and Policy Analysis*, 40(4), 586–612. https://doi.org/10.3102/0162373718785764.

15 For an examination of team cohesion in schools, see Chapter 13 of Sam Crome's *The Power of Teams*.

16 Beal, D. J., Cohen, R. R., Burke, M. J., and McLendon, C. L. (2003). Cohesion and performance in groups: A meta-analytic clarification of construct relations. *Journal of Applied Psychology*, 88(6), 989–1004.

17 Beal, D. J., Cohen, R. R., Burke, M. J., and McLendon, C. L. Cohesion and performance in groups: A meta-analytic clarification of construct relations.

18 A group of science teachers seeking to apply the lessons of cognitive science to science teaching.

4 Mastery

Problem When our development stalls, so does our motivation.	**Solution** Commit to sustainable improvement.

For Zoe, teaching is something 'I always wanted to do, right from being a little girl.' Even when she was in reception, Zoe told people she was going to be a teacher. Then she worked hard to make sure that happened. Whilst friends were 'dropping out' of sixth form, Zoe was 'determined to stay because I wanted to be a teacher.'

The same drive that propelled her into teaching has brought with it a drive to be an effective and constantly improving teacher. 'Teaching is a reflective job. You can't help but look back and sometimes you're your worst critic. You think *I wish I'd done it* that *way.*'

In part, Zoe has driven her own improvement, but she also recognises that, during her nearly 30-year career, staff training has improved dramatically. 'Staff meetings have changed tremendously. They used to be about dates and admin.' Now, she describes how her current headteacher will share some reading or ideas with staff; there will be time to digest these followed by discussion of how to implement them. Zoe has noticed an expectation that more teachers and more schools will engage in research than when she started. 'There's more focus on looking at the theory and putting it into practice.'

There's a humility to Zoe's attitude to professional growth. 'I don't feel I know everything because I've been teaching as long as I have.' What Zoe captures in our brief conversation is a sense of what it is to be a teacher: to constantly feel we're reaching the horizon of our development only to see the next horizon open out before us.

DOI: 10.4324/9781003453154-6

Problem

How have you improved as a teacher in the last year? If you can think of lots of answers to that question, chances are you feel motivated to continue that journey of development. If development feels sluggish, it would be understandable to have less enthusiasm for the job. Whether we feel that we're doing well or improving has a massive impact on our drive to keep going. Looking back, I wasn't really enjoying teaching until I thought I was getting better at it. The more I experienced success, the more I wanted to improve and learn and get better. It sounds obvious, but embedding and retaining those behaviours that work are incredibly motivating.

Thomas Guskey, professor of educational psychology, describes this process: 'Practices that are found to work, that is, those that teachers find useful in helping students attain desired learning outcomes are retained and repeated.'[1]

Too often, though, the work done in schools to improve teaching and teachers has mixed or poor results. Guskey describes the problem with lots of Continuing Professional Development (CPD) in an investigation into the introduction of mastery learning techniques with a group of teachers.[2] Three groups of teachers emerge after receiving training on these techniques:

- Some teachers embed the techniques and see improvement in their students' learning.

- Some teachers tried the techniques but didn't see a noticeable improvement and so dropped them.

- One group didn't adopt or use any of the strategies at all.

For the first group, there was an improvement in teaching but also in outlook; these teachers were actually enjoying teaching more. Bereft of those feelings of accomplishment, the other two groups didn't experience any meaningful change.

The lesson here is not that two thirds of teachers are ineffectual or lazy. Rather, the conditions for successful CPD often haven't been reached, at least not comprehensively. Problems of poor classroom behaviour or time or a lack of clarity around implementation could mean that those second two groups will struggle to introduce the strategies effectively. We can, in this way, feel left behind by work done to improve our teaching.

Has CPD you've engaged with improved your practice? It's a genuine question. I'm sure some has. Not every meeting we go into can have a transformative effect on our teaching. But if the majority feels out of touch or ineffective, we're likely to feel demotivated. Data suggest that many teachers don't find CPD useful: 4 in 10 teachers don't think the way their school spends time on CPD helps them to improve. Almost the same number again don't believe that cancelling Inset (in-service training) for the next five years would have a detrimental impact on their teaching.[3]

Not all improvement occurs within the borders of formal professional development. We drive our own improvement, too. At times, this is rapid; at others, it stalls. Improvement isn't optional, though. It isn't a luxury. When we don't feel that we're getting better, when there aren't opportunities to get better, when there are barriers in our way, we start to lose what we loved about teaching to begin with.

Teachers tend to improve over time but that improvement varies massively between teachers and schools. It's true that teachers tend to improve, on average, as they gain experience, but this average can mask vast differences. In the best schools, those with a rich clear professional development culture, teachers improve much more rapidly than those in schools without such a culture.[4] Sound obvious? But what this means is that our improvement isn't guaranteed. It means that there are teachers out there – you may be one of them – experiencing massive frustration because it doesn't feel like improvement is happening. And it doesn't feel like it's going to happen.

Individual teachers can't change the professional development culture or practices in their school. So what can they do?

Solutions

Anna is a Year 6 teacher, keenly aware of the challenges in taking on a tricky class in an important year. It's October and the class's behaviour isn't what she'd hoped it would be. Pressure from above is mounting not just to sort out behaviour but to ensure a good result in the SATs in the summer. Although this pressure isn't massively helpful, Anna does agree that something needs to change. She just isn't sure what.

As luck would have it, in October Anna must set a professional development goal, one broader area she will work on for the year. After talking to colleagues and the deputy head, Anna settles on fostering independence in her class, driving towards increasingly extended periods where the children can work without significant input.

Underlying this goal is the recognition of the sorts of behaviour Anna wants to develop in her class. When she has to devote long stretches of the lesson to one-to-one or small group support to individuals, behaviour in the rest of the class suffers. Clarifying the goal has also clarified the actions Anna wants to focus on first. If independence is what she's driving at, Anna wants to refine how she scaffolds tasks to gradually hand over that responsibility to the children. She also wants to be clearer with the children about what they can expect from her and what they can't, about when they should ask for help and when they should try their best and perhaps even struggle, if only for a short period.

As Anna begins to work on this, she feels an energy for tackling the big problems in her class that had dwindled pretty rapidly in September. Both the destination, greater independence in her class, and the process, working on various refinements, excite and motivate her.

An attitude of mastery

If *mastery* is the motivator, it could feel clear what we have to do – get better. How we do that is much more difficult. So much is said and done about teacher development that it's hard to unpick how we can harness the motivating power of mastery. Many books have been written, from just about every conceivable angle, about mastering teaching. I won't spend time now rehashing the evidence or ideas about what makes great teaching.[5]

Instead, it's worth considering the position and attitude that make mastery more likely.

To do that, let's look at

- The power of setting goals

- How we set meaningful goals

- Reflection questions to support goal setting

- Tracking our progress

The power of setting goals

Ayelet Fishbach, professor of behavioural science, emphasises the importance of goals in the individual's pursuit of changed behaviour. She describes how 'Powerful goals have the ability to pull us towards our ultimate desires, energizing us to put in the work.'[6] Simply put, clarifying what we want – our goals – motivates us to achieve them.

We should, Fishbach contends, separate our goals from the steps we take to achieve them. A powerful goal should be an 'aspiration, not a chore', a 'desirable state, not the means to get there.' All too easily, the trees can obscure the wood. Getting lost in the 'chore' of practising a single behaviour, forgetting the loftier goal is a real possibility. Much is made in teaching at the moment of the next step, the action we need to take to improve. Practising defined behaviours does improve performance[7] but this isn't what should come first.

How we set meaningful goals

What are your goals as a teacher? To some, this might seem like a strange question. We don't often ask ourselves where we're going. We turn up, teach, and hope to do the same again tomorrow.

Busy teachers are understandably unlikely to create the time to set meaningful goals. There is so much going on. But if we want to change our behaviour, a goal is the place to start.

Fishbach's criteria help us to set meaningful goals. They should be

- **Aspirational**. Ambitious goals can feel at odds with the reality of everyday teaching. Changed behaviour is often won out of the drive to get *somewhere else*. If that place looks vaguely like where we are now or just vague in a way that means we can't really tell where we're trying to get to, action towards our goals will often falter.

- **Abstract first**. We avoid making goals a chore when it's clear that we're not just setting out to complete a list of tasks. Steps that will get us to our goal are essential, but they aren't *of first importance*. Abstract doesn't mean ill defined; these goals simply 'capture the purpose behind an action, describing what you're trying to achieve rather than the actions you'll take to achieve it.'[8] We set a goal to *learn how to explain tricky concepts in History so that students understand them* rather than *Plan better lessons in Cold War unit*. We set a goal to *Promote positive behaviour so that students can self-regulate* rather than *Use the praise-and-consequence system*.

- **Not a means to another goal**. Honesty with ourselves is not always easy. A goal like *Become an expert lesson planner* can sound like the kind of thing we're *meant* to say. We might just want to save time. *Having more time mid-week to spend with friends and family* could be the heart of what we're after.

- **A clear way forward**. Despite starting with the abstract, if we have no clear first steps to achieve it, it is likely to remain a fantasy rather than a goal. In setting our goals, visualising how it might look to achieve them is more likely to lead to success.

Reflection questions for goal setting

I'm going to ask you to set a goal. Rather than just let your mind wander over various half-formed desires, stop and write something down. Use these questions to help you.

What is your destination? Where do you want to get to that is *different from now?*

This could be a teaching behaviour, a way of working or something else. A problem you're facing might prompt your thinking – a difficult class, a lack of motivation, a struggle with a school system – but try, where you can, to set the goal positively.

If behaviour is a problem, we visualise a time when students behave well and define what that looks like. If we're drowning in content, we look ahead to the well-structured, streamlined approach to planning that we're working towards. If we struggle to cater for those in our mixed year group classes, we picture a classroom where all needs are met and all children thrive.

Why is this your destination? What benefits does being in this new place bring?

To justify our goals, we really need to know what we want. Fishbach points out we're more motivated when we can answer *Why?* questions about our goals.

So consider that destination you've just been thinking about. Why do you want to get there? It solves one of the problems we've just been talking about. It improves your abilities in a way that likely improves things for the young people. It fixes your attention on the best bets from research and practice.

An easier life is not a bad justification, but if every goal takes us towards an easier life and none helps us to improve, none addresses the complex problems in our classroom, we might achieve an easier life at the expense of our development.

Is this what you actually want? Or is it a means to something else?

The absence of poor behaviour is slightly different from the presence of positive behaviour. Getting through all the tasks on our to-do list is different from being consistently effective each day. Raising our expectations is not the same as becoming a strict ogre.

Define what you want. Define what is similar to your goal but *not quite it*. What might others confuse your goal for? If you had to explain it, what are you worried a colleague or leader might mistake it for?

Are there any clear ways forward?

If you have a destination but no earthly knowledge of how to get there or how to figure out how to get there, we have a hope or a desire. Not a goal. It isn't that we must have everything figured out as we move towards that destination. Our end point doesn't have to be a fully realised place in our minds. There may be questions, people or resources we need, but that link between the aspiration and the first step is a powerful motivator.

Try setting a goal now. If it helps, frame the goal like this:

By... *Choose a time frame.*
I am/I will... *Choose a goal.*
So that... *Define the desired outcome.*

Tracking your progress

You don't need an unwieldy spreadsheet to track your progress towards a goal, but a system that reminds and refocuses you can be helpful. If we've set a deadline by which we want to have achieved something, defining milestones before that deadline can make achieving the goal more likely.

Anna, our Year 6 teacher, wanted to help her class to work independently more of the time. In a way, she's thinking about this every day, but she recognises the need for focused, uninterrupted reflection. She sets aside time in her calendar to reflect on recent lessons, using student work as an indicator of progress. As she set out to work on her goal, she invites a colleague to come to her classroom and give some feedback. Helpfully, her school's professional development systems encourage this kind of peer collaboration, dedicated meeting time to discuss progress. By the time Anna reaches the date she wanted to achieve her goal, she will have gone through several milestones, including lesson drop-ins from colleagues, reflection by Anna herself, and meeting time.

Tackling the demotivators

I'd understand some scepticism about the core needs of Self-Determination Theory. Isn't it just about behaviour and workload? Perhaps, if we just tackled those things, teachers would be motivated. A wealth of survey data supports the idea that the main push factors from teaching include behaviour, excessive workload, and poor management.[9]

One secondary teacher I spoke to captures how struggles with behaviour can undermine our core needs. 'I don't like feeling powerless. I would say that recently I've felt more powerless than probably ever.' Teaching, to this teacher, 'does make you a control freak'. It heightens our sense of autonomy or lack of it because 'You're supposed to be in control of a room.' She pauses and repeats, 'Supposed to be.' The cause for this feeling is behaviour. Days filled with student defiance are 'particularly draining.' Here, then, we see how feelings of autonomy and mastery might depend on experiences beyond our control. Feelings of relatedness might also suffer as we isolate ourselves in an unwarranted sense of failure.

In which areas do you feel needs are being met? In which do you have control? In which could you work for control? In which could you seek support? Your motivation to teach isn't peripheral. It isn't a *nice to have*. It's core to how we experience each day. If your motivation to teach feels low, spend some time reconsidering the key takeaways from these chapters.

Key Takeaways

- Reflect on your progress. Spend some time writing down the ways you've improved in the last six months. Push it back to a year and then five years, keeping it up in increments for however long you've been teaching. There's a danger that the lack of progress in the recent past is demotivating, but lots of us are blind to the progress we are making until we give it our full attention.

- Set a goal. Goals motivate us. In particular, the connection between the abstract and the specific, between the lofty and the grounded. In the chapters to come, we'll examine how to automate those behaviours, to make those good habits and break a few bad ones. We can only do this in the context of a stronger, greater desire for something more, something we're striving towards. This goal can be personal – I want to be a better spouse, partner, father, mother, friend in X way so I will reduce the time I spend at work – or it can be professional – I will become an expert explainer of tricky physics concepts. Of course, you can do both.

Notes

1 Guskey, T. (2002). Professional development and teacher change. *Teachers and Teaching: Theory and Practice*, 8(3–4), 381–391.
2 Guskey, T. (1985). Staff development and teacher change. *Educational Leadership*, 42(7), 57–60.
3 Teacher Tapp poll data. (2022). Accessed from https://twitter.com/HFletcherWood/status/1727366099275227556 (accessed on 23/11/2023).
4 Kraft, M. A., and Papay, J. P. (2014). Can professional environments in schools promote teacher development? Explaining heterogeneity in returns to teaching experience. *Educational Effectiveness and Policy Analysis*, 36(4), 476–500.
5 It's worth reading, knowing and considering how the following texts apply to your subject or phase:
Teach like a Champion by Doug Lemov.
The Principles of Instruction by Barak Rosenshine.
The Great Teaching Toolkit from Evidence Based Education.
6 Fishbach, A. (2022). *Get it Done*. London: Macmillan.
7 Ericson, A. (2006). The influence of experience and deliberate practice on the development of superior expert performance. In Ericson, A. (Ed.), *The Cambridge Handbook of Expertise and Expert Performance*. Cambridge: Cambridge University Press, pp. 683–704.
8 Fishbach, A. (2022). *Get it Done*. London, Macmillan.
9 For example, Menzies, L., Parameshwaran, M., Trethewey, A., Shaw, B., Baars, S., Chiong, C. (2015). *Why teach?* LKMco Report.

⚓ Sustaining Motivation – Notes for Leaders

Each section in this book will give some notes for leaders based on the research and ideas found in the chapter. Whilst I want teachers to feel empowered to take control of whatever they can, we must recognise that leaders are in a unique position to make things better for staff in their schools. At times, these sections will make suggestions for specific changes; at times, they will ask leaders to understand the unintended consequences of their actions.

A school leader's responsibility is to be obsessed with solving the problems of being a teacher. To do this, the following questions are useful to ask, particularly when evaluating initiatives or introducing something new.

- What problem is X trying to solve? Is this our priority?

- Are we clear enough on why X needs to happen? Can we communicate its importance to staff?

- Have we taken feedback on X from a range of staff?

- Have the possible unintended consequences of X been discussed? Have we considered how we will mitigate for these consequences?

- Have we considered what expectations we will cut back or how we will provide time?

Leaders must obsess over these questions and strive to understand the answers because of the monumental duty they carry. A duty to sustain and maintain a profession that is beset with pressures that will, if we let them, morph and expand the workload, intensity, and stress of the teacher. Don't forget: teachers have the impact; leaders enable it. To what extent are you enabling the teachers you serve to be successful?

Whilst these sections are written *to* leaders, an additional purpose of these sections is to give teachers a bank of ideas, suggestions and knowledge of what could

DOI: 10.4324/9781003453154-7

be done in their schools. Whilst leaders should always do more to listen to their staff, teachers should do as much as they can to feedback, contribute, and suggest ways to improve the ways we work.

Recognise that you have the power to motivate and demotivate your staff (however unintentionally). Staff aren't simply motivated or not. Teachers don't get out of bed in the morning and decide to do a bad job. At times, a bad job is done because they settle for a low standard. But more often, workload or leadership practices constrict and demotivate staff. Deci and Ryan describe how all of us are motivated by autonomy, relatedness, and competence. As a leader, you have distinct and specific control over those things. It's easy to shrug and say, *staff just can't have autonomy over X*. It's harder to actually consider how you motivate and demotivate staff.

Be careful about restrictions to autonomy. Be clear on what staff *must* do. Decide these things carefully and keep them to a minimum. For example, leaders might say that all lessons must start with a silent activity. They might say this because lesson transitions and starts have been identified as an area of concern or friction. This is fine. Be clear with staff about why. Perhaps put a deadline or review point on the common practice.

Where possible, construct policies *with* staff. A feedback policy that mandates a particular type or frequency of feedback, without consulting staff, can lead to a feeling that the policy *doesn't work* before it's even been introduced. Where principles can be mandated and practice is decided by teams or individuals, we make it clear that staff autonomy is important.

Be clear with yourself and with the wider leadership team, every time you make a decision about the way staff *must* do something, you reduce their autonomy (and possibly their motivation for the job). Make these decisions carefully. Be careful too of saying, *Well I've got autonomy; they just aren't exercising theirs*. Those in leadership roles enjoy more autonomy than classroom teachers.[1]

Encourage connections to encourage relatedness. A headteacher I know started their role by appointing a Head of Fun, at least temporarily. When she told me this was her plan, I admit to feelings of cynicism. The Head of Fun would work to create a positive culture among staff by connecting them through events and activities. No one was being forced to 'have fun'. This wasn't mandatory yoga or enforced trips to the pub. Instead, it was engineering of opportunity for staff to spend more time together. This headteacher got something I didn't: these things don't happen by chance, at least not normally. Some schools might have a culture of staff socialising that has grown organically. In schools where this isn't the case, it's unlikely that just waiting for this to happen will lead to success. To what extent do you see your role as creating a positive culture where staff connect?

Harness the power of goals. If a school is implementing something new, leaders must overcommunicate *why* the policy is needed and perhaps *what* problem it solves. Shared goals can make that *why* feel tangible and attainable.

Goals, even broad goals, give us a structure from which we can hang the behaviours we want to see in staff. The relationship between goals and behaviours, therefore, is incredibly important.

We might frame it this way: Goal *therefore* Behaviour.

For example:

- 100% of lessons will start promptly; *therefore*, teachers meet and greet students in the corridor.

- All students will have their thinking checked in every lesson, *therefore*, every lesson will include mini-whiteboards, hands-down questions, or both.

Leaders can too easily skip to the behaviour, believing the goal has been communicated. Maybe it has, but it likely needs communicating regularly rather than once.

Allow freedom in setting professional development goals. When I was a new teacher, I had to fill in this incomprehensible form for 'performance management'. I say I had to fill it in, but, in reality, I had it filled in for me. The type and number of targets I had were mandated, and even the targets themselves were basically chosen for us. After about 11 months, we would remind ourselves of these targets and check if we'd done them and then do some work to prove we had (even when we probably hadn't). My performance wasn't being managed, but it wasn't being developed either.

Thirty-eight percent of teachers say they have 'little' or 'no' influence over professional development goals.[2] Just increasing teacher autonomy over these goals made it more likely that they would stay in teaching and have higher job satisfaction. Too many schools still have arcane performance management processes that do nothing to manage performance, let alone develop it. If this is your school, investigate alternatives now.

Many schools are championing more forward-thinking approaches to performance management. If yours is top-down, heavily reliant on unreliable data, or not teacher-led, seek out and investigate alternatives. If you think you're in the forward-thinking camp, ask staff. Check. Make sure.

Communicate the value. Understandably, where teachers don't see the value in a task, they're going to be unmotivated to do it.[3] That's fine, you might think. We all, from time to time, have to do things that we don't see the value in. But the more we mandate low-value tasks that serve our ability to track, monitor, or over-administrate the running of our school, the more we engender a stagnation of productivity as too much teacher time is given over to non-teaching activities. As leaders, we must be able to communicate the value of something clearly and succinctly or we should stop doing that thing. We should be eagerly open to feedback that a task we see as high-value is not seen the same way by all. We should be open to the conclusion that something that is 'high-value' for leaders is actually something serving *our* needs and not the needs of staff, students, or the school.

If a task has value but is in danger of being perceived as otherwise, your job is to overcommunicate. Briefings, one-on-one conversations, and line management should all be full of a shared message: *this* has value, *this* is why. Limiting the number of these messages given at any time helps, as does sharing the role of communication across a leadership team.

Notes

1 Worth, J., and Van De Brande, J. (2020). Teacher autonomy: How does it relate to job satisfaction and retention? National Foundation for Educational Research Report.
2 Worth, J., and Van De Brande, J. Teacher autonomy: how does it relate to job satisfaction and retention?
3 Feldon, D., Callan, G., Juth, S., and Jeong, S. (2019). Cognitive load as motivational cost. *Educational Psychology Review*, 31(2), 319–337.

PART 2
Managing Intensity

Problem	Solution
Chapter 5 We have to process an overwhelming quantity of information each day.	Develop systems for managing information, messages, and tasks.
Chapter 6 A teaching day is physically and mentally exhausting.	Slow down and do less, better.

DOI: 10.4324/9781003453154-8

5 Intensity of Activity

Problem	Solution
We have to process an overwhelming quantity of information each day.	Develop systems for managing information, messages, and tasks.

Why is teaching so intense? Head of English, Mel, puts it simply but accurately when she tells me, 'It's never done.' But more than that, 'You could literally never sleep and always work and there would still be more to do.' Teaching is clearly like this for everyone, but as Mel points out, it may affect some more than others.

> I'm someone who take my job really seriously. Even when I was working in a pub, I put a lot into it. When you're someone like that and you want to do it really well, teaching can be really difficult because it can be hard to switch off or say *That's enough.*

Mel beautifully captures the tension between the challenge and the joy of intensity. After a stressful few days, Mel explains, '[I] taught my Year 9s who are the most lovely class.' When she'd finished teaching,

> I realised I'd forgotten all of the things that were on my mind that are bothering me. And that's what I get from teaching. It feels like it really cleanses me from everything that's going on. In the moment when I'm teaching, I'm just there; I'm just teaching.

DOI: 10.4324/9781003453154-9

Mel doesn't leave it there but offers an analogy for the intensity of teaching:

> I go [outdoor] swimming in winter – the colder the better – and it's the same feeling. The reason why I love it and why it helps me deal with stress is that when you go into particularly cold water, all you can focus on is that. You're very much in that moment. That's what teaching is like – stepping into ice cold water.

Mel helpfully mentions that this analogy works only 'if you like ice cold water.'

Where does this intensity come from? And how can we, like Mel, thrive on and enjoy it without becoming overwhelmed?

Problem

Work intensity expert, Professor Francis Green, describes intensity as 'the rate of physical and/or mental input to work tasks performed during the working day.'[1] So intensity is the speed and quantity of input during the day that adds to what we have to *do* or *think about* or *decide*. The cognitive demands of being a teacher aren't just about the type of work or handling potentially stressful situations, although teaching definitely includes those. The sheer quantity of information, tasks, requests, and ideas coming your way during the school day, let alone a single lesson, all contribute to an escalating intensity. On top of that, teaching is a physical job: you're standing, moving, and talking for extended periods throughout the day. You're rushing to go on duty or to the loo between lessons; you're carrying boxes of books between rooms.

We know that teaching is intense, but do we know what impact that is having? We need to manage intensity, of course, but what are we managing it for? To put it another way, what happens when we don't manage the intensity of the job?

- Fatigue – Intensity forces us to pay attention to too much; it stretches our attentional resources to and beyond their limit. But 'attention is not costless---the effort required to attend to decisions and execute them well can be costly and cognitively tiring.'[2] We can find ourselves not only physically exhausted by a day's teaching but mentally and emotionally drained too.

- Performance – The intensity of teaching leads us to feel stressed about the quantity of input, about when and whether we'll get it all done, and about whether we'll remember everything we have to do. Research suggests that this stress doesn't simply make us enjoy our job less; it actually makes us worse at what we do.[3]

- Satisfaction – Sometimes, we can look around at the workload and at our experience day to day and think, *This is just what things are like at the moment*, failing to realise that *at the moment* has been our reality for some time. If we want to enjoy and thrive in our working life, if we want to feel satisfied that we're doing a good job or making progress, we need to recognise and deal with the intensity we face.

● Stress – Intensity can prompt stress but also compound it. Stress isn't just background noise in a challenging job. Sustained stress can make you work slower and limit your ability to pay attention for extended periods.[4] Students notice stress in teachers, and they tend to view this as linked to the level of support they receive from teachers.[5] In turn, teachers feel guilty about the all-too-clear consequences of stress.

So we manage intensity, not because intensity is inherently negative but because intensity can bring with it a whole range of negatives we want to avoid. Our experience of, but also our effectiveness at, being a teacher suffers when intensity spirals dangerously beyond our control.

Solutions

Robert, a primary teacher for 12 years, recognises that intensity is driven not just by activity but by the change that seems to characterise teaching. 'I don't think there's been a year where there hasn't been something big introduced. Change is constant.' In this chapter, we'll examine solutions to the quantity of activity inherent to each school day, but, before we do, Robert offers one piece of wisdom that can help to frame what follows: 'You've got to see the reason why each thing is being done.' It's no use managing lots of activity if you don't really get why you're doing it or if you actively feel a task is a waste of time. In cases like this, motivation, as we saw in Part 1, is likely to suffer.

Perhaps unsurprisingly, given what we've heard about intensity, managing the frenetic pace of teaching is about managing our workload. We'll return to workload again in Part 4, but for now let's examine how managing intensity is about the tasks and information we need to consider each day.

To do, make a list

Professor Green describes how feelings of intensity can be alleviated when we can exercise 'discretion' about how we complete tasks.[6] Too often in teaching, it feels like you don't have a choice about how to work, about what you can and can't do. But how messages come through to you, when you manage that information flow, when and how you respond, that is all up to you.

To manage intensity, we need to increase control. A to-do list isn't, in itself, a sign of a person who is in control. Such a list can exist on 12 sticky notes or the torn lid from a box of board pens. The list that is always accumulating adds to our sense of stress rather than diminishes it.

But a list can help with the problems of intensity in a few ways:

● It outsources our thinking, at least for a moment, removing that frantic sense that there's something (or many things) that we are missing.

● It slows down the process by which you respond to the quantity of stuff in each day. Possibly counter-intuitive but this means you can dull that feeling that everything must be done *now*.

● It allows you to sort the items in a way that works for you.

A to-do list can just be that – a list. But we can also explore formats that help to lessen the intensity of the week by organising our tasks a little bit more.
One option is this:

Today	This Week	Hold

On *Today*, I'd add anything that needs to be done before the close of play. Strict adherence to this list is difficult. In teaching, we come to expect the unexpected. A phone call that drags on. An end-of-day conversation commiserating with a colleague who missed out on a promotion.

If an item is not completed that day, we can leave it on there for the next. But be careful of overestimating what is possible in a single day. It's better to complete more from the next list than forever be leaving off items you intended to get done today.

On *This Week*, we collect anything we're trying to achieve during the week. Things we're tasked with – like data entry – and things we want to achieve – like refining our resources from last year for next term's unit. As I plan ahead, I can move things from *This Week* into *Today*.

On *Hold*, we put those items we want to remember – dates, deadlines, upcoming tasks – but don't need to or can't do yet.

I've moved from the model above to something more like this:

Monday	Tuesday	Wednesday	Thursday	Friday

It works the same as the above but allows me to plan my week more thoroughly. I know what I'll be doing each, whether there will be time for extended tasks and when deadlines are. At the end of the week, I look ahead and plan at least the first few days of the next week. During the week, as things come up and change, I update my list. I can reduce the intensity I'm feeling by reviewing tasks and time

I have and pushing some things back a few days to make room for an unexpected job or something taking longer than I'd planned for. This list can be personalised so if you know you can be in early or stay a bit later on certain days, you can add "AM" or "PM" as headings to specifically book things into those times. "PPA" (planning, preparation, and assessment) can become another heading. Equally, you can populate this table with your lessons, and specific tasks for lessons – collecting in homework, giving out messages – can be put next to the lesson itself. Of course, your planner or calendar can serve a similar function, but I like the flexibility of being able to move tasks around as the week happens.

Another classic approach is the Eisenhower Matrix:

	Urgent	**Not Urgent**
Important	Do	Schedule
Not Important	Delegate	Don't

The matrix asks us to organise our tasks by the urgency and importance. This matrix is particularly useful when we find ourselves in a situation where we have more than feels possible to complete. If you're swamped, pause and populate it with everything you have to do right now:

- *Urgent* is determined by deadline. When is this work due? Teaching is beset with the urgent. Lessons to plan. Feedback to give. Phone calls to return.

- *Important* is harder to pin down. *Important* for whom? It's your list so you get to decide. Importance could be determined by what will have the biggest impact. Which of your nearly infinite options is the lever to pull? Which one will make learning more likely, more effective, or more efficient?

Both *Urgent* and *Important* can be seen from one more useful perspective. *Urgent* and *Important* for how many? How many members of staff? How many parents? Most importantly, how many students? We can use these and the questions above to rate and compare the tasks we find ourselves overwhelmed by.

Deliberate planning of lessons is more likely to shape successful learning than making a phone call to a single parent. Often, of course, we're able to do both, but the comparison is helpful in forcing us to honestly appraise the value in the tasks we do.

Does this mean you never make the phone call? No, but to decide what we're going to do at the end of a day, we can ask the following questions.

- Does the call *have to* happen? Does it have to happen *now*?

- *To answer the question above, we might ask*: Is this something you've decided to do? Or been directed to do?

- If it's something you've decided to do, is it *essential* or *nice to have?* Can it wait? If so, let it wait. Book it in for a time you know you can do it later.

- If it's been directed, by an individual or a policy?

You're sitting at the desk in your classroom, keen to go home but with two items left on today's to-do list:

- Adapt resources, lesson 12 pp – Year 8 Wed P1

- Feedback sheets Year 8

The tasks concern the same lesson. What questions can we ask of these tasks to understand which to devote the time to.

- We could ask *What needs to happen by tomorrow morning?* And we might think that the resources take precedence. That's the basis of our lesson; it needs to be ready.

- But we could also ask *What's going to have the biggest impact on learning?* The question isn't so clearcut, but the feedback is going to address misconceptions and errors students have in their work.

We decide to do the feedback because that will plan some of the following lesson anyway. Instead of ignoring the need to adapt the resources, we'll devote a shorter chunk of time (about ten minutes) to that in the morning. It's not that this is the 'right' answer. It only, hopefully, serves to illustrate the alternative to frantically trying to do everything before you leave.

A note on delegate or don't

I'm just *a teacher*, you might say, *I can't delegate and I can't say no to what I'm asked to do.*

If the headteacher asks you to do something, you probably have to do it, but here are some ways of moving towards not doing something or even of delegating it:

- We've been asked to do X, Y, and Z this week. Which is the priority because I'm not sure it's feasible to do all?

- The data needed on your management information system (MIS) has already been put into Excel. Is there any admin capacity to transfer it over?

- I'm feeling a bit overwhelmed by the quantity I've got to get done at the moment. Can I just share my list with you and check if there's anything that can wait?

There is power in asking the person making the demands of you to prioritise.

The power of *Don't* when we really take hold of it can be profound. The only way to really reduce intensity and workload is to be happy to do fewer things (more on this in the next chapter). We'd like to evolve homework into something more useful, but we don't have time at the moment. It goes on hold or we recognise the jobs we hoped to get done will, for now at least, have to be removed from our list altogether. We've spent our career to date making resources for all lessons and classes from scratch. We realise this is what is driving the intensity of everything else and decide to stop, focusing on improving our ability to adapt the resources our team shares.

A note on to-do items

Intensity, we've seen, is driven by the quantity of new information that comes to us each day. A to-do list doesn't help when it doesn't define, with some granularity, what you need to do. If you have to start, figuring out how to complete a task, every time you look at your list, it isn't working.

A to-do list outsources some of your thinking – you don't need to hold those things in your head anymore – but should also make starting and completing tasks more straightforward – when you sit down to work through your list, you know exactly that is needed.

Poor to-do list items include

- Marking

- Plan Year 8

- Complete data sheet

- Set homework

These are poor items because they don't define specifically what is going to be done. You will arrive at them in a PPA or before school having to do the mental activity of what needs to be done next.

Your to-do list should have done some of the thinking for you. So, instead, consider items like this:

- Fill in whole class feedback sheet for 8x based on sample of 10 books.

- Check with Jen if we are still using resources in y drive for Circuits unit

- Plan Thursday P1

- Check all marks for end-of-topic test (9y2)

- Enter marks into Sims by Friday 8 a.m.

Depending on what style of list we're making, we can then organise these in terms of importance in our list. Notice that each item starts with a verb. Each is a distinct and doable action. Just starting with a verb doesn't solve all of our problems. We could write *Plan next term's lessons* or *Solve disagreement between Ella and Rosie*, items that it's unlikely we can solve in one go.

Email

If you're a headteacher, you're likely to send and read more emails than anyone else. Class teachers send the fewest emails, but, on average, they still receive 10 or more emails each day, with many receiving lots more.[7] You have fairly little control over how many emails you receive. You do have control over how you respond to them.

Too often, I've had my email open on my screen with the notification noise on and just let it interrupt my day. This isn't just an interruption; it's another input, another call for my attention. Even when I'm teaching, I've stopped to check emails because the ding of the computer has called me to it with something like Pavlovian instinct. All this just serves to add to the intensity of your day as you try to juggle the demands of *what you were doing* with the new information or instruction that comes at you via email.

What can you do to manage email and lessen intensity?

- **Turn off the notifications**. Don't let a computer direct your attention. Keep control of where you focus. If you're in the middle of planning or marking or meeting someone or even teaching, you can ensure your focus on the task at hand by eliminating distractions. You might feel the pull to know what's going on as soon as you can, but so little of what comes through via email has the kind of value that warrants this kind of response.

- **Close the email app**. In my experience, this is a difficult but rewarding strategy. It's difficult because we don't want to do it. It's difficult because, for a lot of us, we have automated a habit to open and keep checking our email even when we're expecting nothing in particular. If you're teaching or working on something you want to focus on, close the browser.

- **Schedule email slots**. We'll talk more about how you structure your day when we discuss workload. If you've closed the browser in the times you wanted to focus on something else, you can now schedule times you focus particularly on email. These should be short bursts of attention you give to email. This might be any time left in the PPA when the more important work is completed. It might be the start of the day after you've set up your classroom. It might be the last thing 15 minutes before you leave. Starting to do this, you can feel like you're missing out. But really, for those of you like me who've become email-obsessed, it's just about giving email attention in proportion to its importance.

● **Don't over-organise**. Some people are obsessed with keeping their inbox at zero or having complicated systems for organising emails. These may work, particularly for those receiving 50-plus emails a day but otherwise seems unnecessary. Your inbox keeps hold of your emails long after you've forgotten about them, and search can locate emails rapidly whether they're in a folder you've made for that topic or not.

● **Manage your responses**. Although each email we receive is different, there are only a handful of ways we're going to respond. Let's work through those now.

  a. **Ignore**. Lots of emails require nothing from you. If it's clear from an email's contents or subject line that I need to do nothing, I delete it immediately so I'm not distracted by that email again in the future.

  b. **Schedule and retain**. Some email comes with important information but doesn't require an immediate response: deadlines, meetings, messages to relay. Adding these as events to your calendar or items on a to-do list makes sure the message is retained without your having to worry about *just remembering* the email.

  c. **Short response**. If an email requires a yes, no, or short answer or if it will take only a minute to respond, respond immediately (in your scheduled slot). Whenever we close the loop on a message or task we've been given, we're removing one of those things vying for our attention, one of those things adding to the intensity of our day.

  d. **Long response**. A small number of emails require a longer, more considered response. If we just try to hold onto the thought – *I need to respond to that* – we'll end up distracted by it, worrying that we'll forget. Put it on your to-do list and it becomes a task we can devote some more focused time to.

  e. **Face to face**. When an email needs a response but it would be easier to speak in person, wait to speak in person. Have the conversation on duty before briefing as you're walking in the next day. Email begets more email. Don't create that chain of misunderstanding by just firing back a reply that isn't quite clear. Go and speak to someone. You'll probably save time in the moment – the issue will be solved – but this way of working saves time in the long term as you send and receive fewer emails.

A final note on email: in some schools, there is a tendency to expect replies to emails almost immediately. An email is sent during period 1 and the hurried, harried sender accosts you at break to ask, 'Have you seen that email?' This approach to email raises the question, *Why don't we just talk to each other more?* If the break-time conversation was going to happen anyway, maybe it would have been a better vehicle to convey the message or ask the question. Be the change you want to see in your school by creating clear boundaries around what is realistically expectable – *I'm free P4;*

I'll be checking email then... I've got to run at the end of the day, so in all honesty I won't be able to look at it until first thing tomorrow morning. Could we talk about it now instead? Email can give the appearance of working at a fast pace when, more often, it's obfuscating rather than clarifying. Slow down your response and see what happens.

Meetings

Meetings and briefings in school are held in contempt by so many teachers and you can see why. Watching people read messages they already shared by email in a PowerPoint that doesn't seem remotely familiar to them can be eye-clawingly painful.

I once sat in a meeting about building work that was going to start across the school. With admirable brevity, the head laid out the plans for the work. Then she made a fatal mistake by offering two words you never want to hear at the end of the meeting, 'Any questions?' What followed was an insight into the deranged psyches of some of my colleagues as they asked increasingly bizarre questions. *Will there still be plug sockets at the back of my room? Will the builders move the tables and chairs into my new room? What will the room be called? Will the dimension of time still exist in my room* (because it had ceased to exist in any real way in that school hall)?

To this day, I don't know if this was a prank with the aim of prompting some kind of violent outburst from me. It came pretty close. I ended up biting down hard into my knuckles to avoid screaming, 'Does no one else want to go home!?'

Meetings suffer from the problem of not defining clearly the purpose. School meetings can and do have a variety of purposes:

- Information sharing

- Discussion and decision making

- Training and development

Lots of meetings try to do more than one of those things. And sometimes one becomes the other before our eyes.

A deputy head was sharing a school's new no-phones policy – clearly information-sharing – when staff started pointing out potential issues, loopholes, and gaps in the policy – discussion and decision making. A short meeting became a long one because the information being shared hadn't been stress-tested first. A quick email survey seeking feedback or lunchtime chat with a few colleagues would have highlighted and rectified the problems straight away.

Meetings add to the intensity of the teaching day when they broadcast more that teachers need to do and think about without giving them the space to do and think about those things. Because you don't necessarily have control over what meetings happen and how they are conducted, it can feel like there isn't much you can do. But there are a few things:

- **Bring your to-do list**. Reduce the intensity of information-sharing meetings by adding any tasks, dates, or deadlines directly to your to-do list.

- **Bring your planner or planning**. If I'm running a meeting, I like people to listen rather than tap away at their emails. If I'm attending, I try to be present by closing the laptop where I can and giving my full attention. So I'm not suggesting you just plough on through your work, ignoring everything going on around you. At times, leaders will ask you to embed something new into lessons, a bit of vocabulary, a technique or strategy. It won't always be possible, but instead of applying this to a theoretical situation, apply it to the real lessons you have coming up.

- **Ask if you need to be there**. This one can feel like the shirker's habit, trying to get out of anything asked of them, but so much of what is discussed in a meeting is relevant to a slice of the staff body. And yet the message or the training is delivered to all. If you see a meeting that doesn't look relevant to you, be bold and ask to skip it. That might look something like

I've noticed the meeting looks geared mainly towards Year 11 teachers. As I don't teach Year 11, can I skip it?

- **Give feedback**. You might think it's not your place. It's not *your* job to tell *them* how to do their jobs. But you have to experience the meetings, which makes your perspective on them useful and important. But start a conversation that goes something like this:

Can I just talk to you about our meetings? I've noticed we share a lot of information and jobs that need to get done, but that information is replicated elsewhere – emails, briefings. It feels to me that we could free up some time for teachers if we thought more about what we do in meetings that is doubling up other work.

We dampen the fires of intensity when we create systems that help us to manage tasks and information. A to-do list won't necessarily put out the fire, but it will help to control the spread.

Key Takeaways

- Intensity can be measured as 'the rate of physical and/or mental input to work tasks performed during the working day.'

- This means how you take on new information and process and store it are all going to, at least in part, determine the intensity of your day.

- Three problems of task management are

  ○ How you collate the information you receive

  ○ The dysfunctional way many in schools use email

  ○ The meeting cycle that adds to teacher workload and reduces teacher time to work

- Systems can respond to them. A to-do list helps to organise the information. It doesn't reduce tasks (more on workload in Part 4), but it helps you to appraise them honestly.

- If you use a to-do list, reflect on how well it works for you. Does it help to manage or add to the intensity of the school day?

- If you don't, trial one. Use one I've suggested here but check back after a week. Has it helped? Adapt it to what you need.

- Think about how you could be more disciplined in your use of email. Choose one step mentioned above and try it out this week.

Notes

1 Green, F. (2001). It's been a hard day's night: The concentration and intensification of work in late twentieth-century Britain. *British Journal of Industrial Relations*, 39(1), 53–80.

2 Archsmith, J., Heyes, A., Neidell, M., and Sampat, B. (2021). The dynamics of inattention in the (baseball) field. Institute of Labour Economics Discussion Paper Series.

3 Altindag, O. (2020). Relationship between stress management and job performance in organizations. *Research in Business and Social Science (2147–4478)*, 9(2), 43–49.

4 Angelidis, A., Solis, E., Lautenback, F., van der Does, W., and Putman, P. (2019). I'm going to fail! Acute cognitive performance anxiety increases threat-interference and impairs WM performance. *PLoS One*, 14, e0210824. https://doi.org/10.1371/journal.pone.0210824.

5 Carroll, A., York, A., Fynes-Clinton, S., Sanders-O'Connor, E., Flynn, L., Bower, J. M., Forrest, K., and Ziaei, M. (2021). The downstream effects of teacher well-being programs: Improvements in teachers' stress, cognition and well-being benefit their students. *Frontiers in Psychology*, 12, 689628.

6 Green, F., Felstead, A., and Henseke, G. (2022). Working still harder. *LR Review*, 75(2), 458–487.

7 TeacherTapp. (2023). The email equation. Accessed from https://teachertapp.co.uk/articles/the-email-equation-calculating-the-workload-of-teachers-inboxes/ (accessed on 30/10/2023).

6 Intensity of the School Day

Problem A teaching day is physically and mentally exhausting.	**Solution** Slow down and do less, better.

When I ask Mel, our Head of English, how intense her day is, her reply is one recognisable to lots of teachers. 'On a scale of 1 to 10 it's a 10. It's feeling like I'm spinning lots of plates.' For Mel, it's a combination of a busy timetable, Head of Department duties, lunchtime clubs, and after-school revision sessions. Busyness isn't entirely a negative in Mel's mind; she thrives on it, acknowledging that 'Teaching is cracking… because there's not really a moment to think about anything else.'

Mel recognises that experience has won her a slightly easier life – 'the longer you teach, the quicker things [can get done]' – but it isn't just an increased rate of work that has made Mel's life easier; it's a change in attitude. 'I've learned that good enough is good enough. It doesn't have to be perfect.' Mel isn't philosophising. A change in attitude has led to a change in approach. She will prioritise, saying 'no to things a lot more' than she used to. If she absolutely has to do something that she doesn't see the value in – an unfortunate reality for teachers – she says, 'I'll get it done when I get it done.'

Like a lot of teachers, Mel has a history of working long and late. As something of a workaholic, she finds it hasn't come naturally to her, but she's decided to 'become much stricter about what I take home' and 'what time I leave.' It's not that Mel's stopped taking work home. She's created a simple rule for herself: 'I only take home things that I enjoy doing.' She'll make resources, particularly the booklets that make up her English curriculum, because she explains 'I love doing that'.

Mel's day is still busy. It's still intense. But it feels more manageable. Let's consider how that could be the case for more of us.

DOI: 10.4324/9781003453154-10

Problem

Teaching isn't just intense because of the quantity of tasks and information to process.

If you think about the mental input during a typical day for a typical teacher, it's massive:

- Before school, there are the emails, the briefing messages, and the corridor conversations.

- During the day, lessons aren't just about teacher delivery to students; students give information to teachers through behaviour, the work they complete, what they say and do (and sometimes what they don't say or do).

- After school, we call parents, prepare for the next day, attend meetings, and more. So, by the end of the day and after our lessons are over, we've had still more inputs added to the tasks we have to complete.

- Contained within all the above are spikes of intensity – diffusing the playground dispute, managing defiance in the classroom, having a difficult phone call, being present at an end-of-day meeting.

The intensity of teaching does not seem to be lessening. In 2017, 9 out of 10 teachers agreed that their job 'required them to work very hard', increasing from around half of teachers in 1992. Only about half of the rest of the working population felt that they were required to work 'very hard'.[1]

Teaching isn't just intense in the short term. Its intensity extends across terms, often barging through our evenings and weekends and intruding on holidays. Teaching days aren't simply intense as one-off, self-contained moments in time. The intensity of the previous day has a direct effect on the intensity of *this* day.

If we aren't careful, we can nurture a feast-or-famine mindset. We know we're living through difficulty; we know we aren't thriving, but we look to the holidays as a time to recuperate. Rest will come, but later. That mindset gets us used to a way of working; we accept a level of intensity where we can't do our best work or our best thinking, where *life* can become overrun by *the job*.

The wrong kind of intensity

We wouldn't have accurately captured teaching if intensity was just a kind of busyness. Quantity of intense activity is an issue, but so is type of intensity. Here, behaviour comes into the foreground. And for many of us, behaviour is in the foreground of our thinking about what it is to be a teacher each day. That class. That student. The lessons tilting on the precipice of a chaotic abyss.

All teachers will have experienced feelings about behaviour that drift up and down a scale from dull awareness through to serious stress. The solutions below can indirectly help with behaviour: they can make us pause, reflect, and slow down. But they aren't behaviour management strategies. That's the problem with behaviour as the cause of intensity in our working days and weeks. It isn't always about a classroom strategy or solution that can solve the problem.

Consider where you are on that behaviour scale at the moment. A one-off bad lesson can leave you frazzled and feeling useless, but it can also be laughed off and commiserated over with colleagues. More regular disruption might be addressed by seeking advice from colleagues, requesting support from leaders, or engaging in Continuing Professional Development.

If, instead, the behaviour is an all-consuming, overwhelming stress that you can't escape even when at home, perhaps prompted by an individual student or class, then support should be sought out as soon as possible. If that support has been requested (perhaps several times and in various ways) and the situation is not improving or if your feelings about behaviour have been made light of, it might be time to look for a school where proper support is available.

The solutions about intensity offered below don't offer behaviour management advice,[2] but they should help whether we're feeling the physical intensity of the school day, the sense of pressure from our to-do list or the stress from an individual's behaviour. They should help with the inevitable results of having to deal with difficult behaviour on a regular basis.

The right kind of intensity

There is perhaps one other angle from which to examine intensity before we move on. A paradoxical thing about intensity is that, at the right level, it can be one of the rewarding bits of the job. There is an excitement, thrill even, in working through a day which is manageably intense. If you enjoy the speed or the variety that teaching affords you, we aren't seeking to get rid of those things. Simply to manage them well.

Once I had to cover for the Head of English over a period of absence. I had to set cover for her lessons but also cover some of her jobs as head of department. I worked in a frenzy, frantically listing everything I needed to do and then attacking that list with enthusiasm. After a couple of days like that, I was surprised by two things. First, the quantity of work completed was far more than I'd usually get done for myself. Second, I quite enjoyed it.

The purpose of this chapter is not to suck out the energy and enjoyment from your day or your term. Intensity can be something we enjoy. The word *managing* is crucial. To what extent are you *managing* intensity? And to what extent are you being swept away by it? The solutions offered aim to help you with the intensity that is unwanted and unsustainable.

Solutions

Because of wider leadership responsibilities, Mari works busier days than a lot of other Heads of History. From duties to lessons to more duties and revision sessions and meetings, it might seem impossible to slow down during these days or to find a time to pause. It's true that Mari isn't having a long lunch or a lot of breaks, but she does think about and prepare for such intensity. She's in early and any makes sure things like photocopying are done before the busyness of the school day starts. Mari also teaches A-Level and tells me that, 'although it is intense in terms of academic content, there are different lull points in a lesson where the students are completely engrossed so I can take a breath.'

Perhaps Mari's view of teaching and teenagers helps her to see break duty as at least a kind of break. 'I think teenagers are brilliant. They look at the world from a completely different viewpoint to adults. They still have a desire to make everything fun.' Break duty, then, lets you see individuals in a 'completely different light.' On break duty, 'Lads that sometimes are causing a ruckus around the school will come to me on duty to have a conversation about my lunch box. We chat about the best crisps.' My point here is not that you should find rest or pause in standing in the cold or the rain as Mari seems to. Rather, it's that both how we organise and how we view our day can have a dramatic effect on feelings of intensity.

Is *less* possible?

Most of the solutions in this section seek to disrupt the intensity of the school day by slowing down and doing less. Intensity festers when we feel the need for perfection in every task, in every moment of every day. It can feel like an impossible task to slow down or do less.

We're going to focus in this section on intensity on the slowing of the teaching day. When we examine workload, we'll return to consider how to do less. I recognise how unhelpful it can be to simply tell a teacher to do less. Less of what? Less of the jobs that make up teaching, the essentials? Less of the things that have been demanded of me by leaders or a head teacher?

Is the idea of reducing just out-of-touch and unrealistic advice then? Hopefully, not. But it does often require that we change our attitudes to work and tasks.

Before we get to doing less, let's consider how we can slow the day down.

Consider how and where you work

We've all met the teacher who complains about how busy they are and yet spends PPA (planning, preparation, and assessment) time gossiping. It's not that you can't or shouldn't enjoy times with others when you aren't teaching. They make the job what it can and should be: collaborative, connected, and fun. But how we work in those PPA times matters, and what is going on around us matters too.

There's some evidence that the more challenging the task, the more we are disrupted when noise interrupts our work.[3] Being able to direct sustained attention at a task or activity is essential for us to be successful and effective, but sustaining attention can lead to fatigue and this fatigue can lead to error or substandard work.[4] Our problem, however, is not simply *paying attention*; it's avoiding the distractions of the school environment. As cognitive scientist Daniel Willingham points out, distraction has both a time-lag and an error cost: we take more time to restart a task, and we're more prone to errors as we restart.[5]

With all this in mind, we need to think seriously about *how* and *where* we work. If you're working on something that requires deep focus, free from distraction – planning a difficult topic, say, or exam marking – choose somewhere you won't be interrupted. This might be a classroom if it's free, but, if your classroom is in a busy part of the school (or next door to music), you'll find it difficult focus there. Staff rooms vary between schools. Some are always almost empty. Others are lively, full of colleagues, breeding grounds for distractions.

If none of the places mentioned offers respite from distraction, you might consider when you do certain kinds of work. If you're in early and before others, you can plan to do those tasks then. The same is true if you're in later than others. Devote this time to the jobs that require your attention to be undivided. Perhaps there's a topic you're teaching that you've taught a thousand times before. You can do this with some distraction. But a new topic, where your subject knowledge is patchy, demands more from you cognitively. You place this planning in a slot you know will be relatively calm.

Of course, you could do all of the above and still feel like you don't have the time you need to truly focus on things. If that's because distraction-free time and space is scarce in your school, talk to leaders. If you work in a subject or phase office, this might be a middle leader. Go with a solution if you've got one. If a space in the school is free, suggest it as a quiet work area.

Rest

Breaks are important for two reasons:

We work better after a break. Breaks seem to replenish our capacities to pay attention and perform.[6] When we take breaks, we make it more likely that will be able to refocus on complexity when we return from our breaks. We may even make better decisions after a break, with our poorest decisions coming at the end of a long period of work *before* a break.[7]

We make it more likely we can work effectively through the day if the day is punctuated with breaks. The idea that your day needs to include some time off work isn't that ground-breaking or controversial, but often teachers will offer entirely valid objections to the idea of taking breaks.

Objection 1: I don't have time. This may be true, but it shouldn't be. We should work against this reality, believing that it's possible to have time to take a break.

We can work at this from two angles: first, we're likely to work better and more efficiently after a break; second, we *should* have time. The idea that you should have to charge through the day, ignoring luxuries like going to the toilet or having a sip of water, is not a healthy way to view teaching.

When I was Head of English, I started just sitting in our department workroom at lunch and eating my lunch. Over time, these became the moments when we stopped as a team, had a chat, moaned, commiserated, celebrated, and enjoyed – for the most part – each other's company. I struggled at that school with behaviour, with leading effectively, and with lots of other things, but the breaks in my day stemmed the rising tide of stress in a way trying to get more done could not have.

Objection 2: No one else is. Sometimes, an incredibly unhelpful culture creeps into a school where it is normal to at least feign surprise that a colleague is having a break or not rushing through every minute of the day. In these schools, it's not uncommon to hear similar comments when colleagues leave school before some unsaid time. At times, dealing with this kind of objection is simply about leading a quiet rebellion where you and a friendly colleague deliberately break to have lunch or coffee. At others, the atmosphere in a school can be more toxic; your deliberate practice of breaks is criticised, or snarky comments are made about being a 'part-timer'. If this is the case, leaders need to hear about the culture in their school – even if those leaders are the ones creating this toxicity.

We increase job satisfaction, wellbeing, and general happiness when we connect with others. If the above suggestions about where and when to work make you feel like a silence-loving killjoy, we need to talk about how breaks *with others* are vital to the reduction of intensity. As researchers into teacher wellbeing point out, 'positive functioning is not simply surviving stress; it also entails thriving physically, mentally, socially, and professionally.'[8]

No teacher is an island. If all we do is manage the information and tasks coming our way, we might get through the day a little easier. We might be surviving, but it's unlikely we'll be thriving. Breaks make life better as we connect with others because we're reminded that we're part of something bigger than ourselves; we remind ourselves that others face the same challenges we do. Perhaps more importantly, we distract ourselves in the best possible way from the busyness or intensity of the day. We increase the sense of relatedness in our work, a key driver of our motivation. For a brief moment, the loneliness of teaching dissipates.

Recover

It's easy to see how what happens either side of our school day can affect how intense that day feels. It's harder to know what to do to manage or reduce that intensity. What's clear is that time outside of school – evenings, weekends, days off, and holidays – are crucial to managing intensity. Recovery time outside of work is linked to better long-term wellbeing and health as well as reduced stress.[9]

The inverse is also true: no recovery time after or between work sessions is likely to increase stress and reduce wellbeing.

Satisfying our basic psychological needs – Deci and Ryan's relatedness, competence, and autonomy – when outside of work has a positive impact when we're next in work, with activity at the weekend playing a particularly important role in this recovery. You can see where this is heading. To manage intensity, teachers can't work every evening or through every weekend. When we work in this way, we believe we're helping *future me* because *I won't have so much to do tomorrow or this weekend*. But this isn't quite right; the research suggests we're likely to make *future me* more stressed and less happy and ultimately less healthy if we continue at such a relentless pace.

What, then, should we do?

Leave work at work. It's easy to say and harder to do. Perhaps our aim should be to leave more work at work. In some ways, I'm a hypocrite: I do send the odd email when at home. I do have email on my phone because I like it there – for the most part – so I know what's going on. Notifications are turned off. But this is a trade-off. I've rarely done planning at home and only done marking in those busy times when books and papers are piling up. What more could you leave? How could you get to the point where you do less?

Leaving work at work is more a mindset than it has to be a definitive demarcation. Cal Newport, writer of *Deep Work* and expert in effective working practices, suggests having an end-of-the-day 'shutdown ritual', a routine that definitively ends the day for you. Newport encourages us to end each day by reviewing every 'incomplete task, goal or project'. We then need to make sure we have a plan for the completion or continuation of all of those things.[10] If it helps, write a list of things you need to remember for the following day. Make the first thing you do to review the list. In the full version of this practice, you can then forget about work until the following day. Don't check email. Don't log on. Don't do anything work-focused. In a partial version of this practice, we may define certain things we'll do or certain times we will work at home. We might, for example, check our email or do some planning (an activity we enjoy).

Put off perfectionism. A problem with teaching is that it is never done. A problem with (and a virtue of) a lot of teachers is that they are perfectionists. In order to *Leave work at work*, we're going to have to accept that certain things cannot be done to the standard we'd want in one day or perhaps at all.

When we spoke, Robert, a primary teacher and leader, reflected on how teaching had changed since he was training. He explained, 'As you become more experienced you find efficiencies or short cuts.' His point is that you need to be willing to take those short cuts:

> As the trainee teacher, you might spend six hours preparing a lesson. You just can't do that for long. You just need to park it. And recognise *There's an 80% solution and that's enough. That's what I've got to go with because I've got lots of other things to do.*

A perfectionist is often unwilling to make compromises or divert towards the shorter route, but, as Robert points out, it's essential if you want to manage the large quantities of stuff in each school day.

Here are some questions that perfectionists can ask as they endeavour to leave work at work:

Is this good enough? If we're not a perfectionist, this is a dangerous question to ask. We can lower our standards and accept less than we should. Perfectionists can ask this as they continue to tinker with a project or task long after they could have finished.

Can this wait? Perfectionists want to complete everything *now*. Their work day starts early and ends late. Lots of that day contains essential activity: teaching, break duty, planning for the following day. But some of that day is filled with extras. Things we want to devote more of our time to or the things we enjoy. It's ok to get things done on the deadline rather than weeks before. It's ok to prioritise one aspect of your practice and ignore another at least for the time being.

Reclaim evenings and weekends. Reflect on your working patterns. If you already rarely work at home, you can skip to the next step. If you work every evening or weekend and it doesn't feel possible to stop all at once, you might want to start by taking back some of that time. Define one or two days in the week when you will work in the evening. List the tasks you're hoping to accomplish in that time.

If it helps, leave a laptop at work. Or tell your partner or housemate that you're not working this evening. It might help even more to try the next step.

Book activities that support recovery. Remember that Deci and Ryan said that we are motivated by autonomy, relatedness, and competence. Engaging with activities where we feel each of those motivators has a refreshing effect on us as we return to work. Meeting the need for autonomy, relatedness, and competence *outside* of work is likely to reduce stress and increase wellbeing when we're *at* work. We can fall into the trap of thinking that recovering from an intense day at work is about sitting in a darkened room and trying to forget about tomorrow, but there's some evidence that activity, activity tied to Deci and Ryan's core motivators, can make all the difference.

I have never wanted to do anything other than watch TV until about 9 o'clock and then head quickly to bed. Engaging with other activity requires intentional effort and planning. Not because we don't want to do these things but because when it gets to 8 o'clock on a school night, the thought of going out feels maddeningly self-defeating –

Do I really want to spend tomorrow tired and miserable?

But when I've followed this advice myself, I've found that I feel more like a 'real person', one of those people who do things in the week, meet friends, and perhaps even have a bit of a life. When I've got to the pub quiz or met a friend for dinner or booked a regular meet-up, I've managed to do it, but, more than that, it made my week feel more enriching and less relentless.

It's not even that you have to leave your house. Deci and Ryan's *competence* motivator could relate to a hobby or a skill you're learning, something completely unrelated to work. It could be reading, a Duolingo habit, or a craft obsession. I love cooking, but sometimes I feel like I should save cooking and baking projects for the weekend. Last night, I made pesto for dinner *on a weeknight.* It felt if not illicit then certainly an extravagant activity for a Wednesday. If I'm honest, I started tired and grumpy, annoyed with myself for choosing *this* meal for *this* day. As I got into it, I focused on the process and was lost in it. I was satisfied in a way that turning on the microwave probably can't achieve *for me.* It's not that you now must make pesto on a weeknight. No, you just have to figure out what distracts, enriches, and fulfils the time you spend not at work.

It's unlikely that just wanting to do something fun or different on a weeknight is going to automatically make it happen, particularly if this is not the norm for you. Calendar activities that take you away from work and towards *relatedness, competence, and autonomy.* Wanting to run regularly probably won't have the same effect as joining a running club. Your desire to learn French will more likely be fulfilled if you sign up for a class. If you want to cook pesto mid-week, you need to plan for it. (I mean, who has pine nuts just sitting in their cupboard?)

Prioritise time outside. Research suggests that time spent in a natural setting can 'mitigate stress' and help to refresh our ability to pay attention.[11] Being outside for extended periods is also linked to reflection and problem-solving.[12] Because our ability to pay attention wanes with extended exertion, a natural environment – where we don't need to pay attention to much of anything – can help to refresh our ability to pay attention. There are also tentative signs that walking helps with problem-solving and thinking creatively.[13]

Reclaim your commute. More time, particularly in the car, to and from work seems to add to the intensity and maybe frustration of each day. Research suggests that 'longer commutes create stresses at work and home that reduce job satisfaction and connection to the workplace.'[14] Longer commutes also make it more likely that you'll look for a job elsewhere. Negative feelings about a commute will probably come to be associated in our minds with our work.[15]

Whilst we can factor this into how we choose future jobs (or where we live), it's not something we can necessarily change right now. But the underlying problem of the bad commute is a problem that we all will face, whether we drive to work or not. To what extent do those times before and after school refresh and reenergise us for the next day at work (or the weekend)? To what extent are those times just extensions of the workday?

Aside from dramatically changing where we live or work, we can do two things to combat this:

Active commuting. That your commute has an impact on your day hardly needs saying. We've all sat in traffic, tired eyed, longing for home and increasingly frustrated we're not getting there. But different modes of commuting can affect us differently. The shorter the drive, the better we feel about our day and even our work.

If, however, we can commute actively – walking or cycling – or pair one of those modes with public transport, our wellbeing increases. An active commute is, of course, a luxury unavailable to many teachers, but adding a walk to your commute where possible or cycling once a week can, perhaps unexpectedly, make you feel better about your work.[16]

Purposeful commuting. Surprisingly, to me at least, people reported higher levels of wellbeing when travelling by public transport compared with travelling by car.[17] It might be possible to mitigate the cost of a stressful commute by diverting the how that time is used to an activity that can bring you joy or fulfil a need or desire. An investigation into 'me time' during commutes found the potential to increase wellbeing and even satisfaction with our jobs by spending commuting time more purposefully.[18] The researchers point out helpfully that you can't read a book whilst cycling or do some woodwork on the train but you can engage in other activities, particularly learning focused activities. You can read. You can learn a language. You can write poetry if you want to. Like those activities we book into our evenings, anything we can do that takes us away from work and towards personal fulfilment is, unsurprisingly, good for us.

If we want the intensity of our work, day to day, to change, we need to change something. The suggestion to choose a more active method of commuting or to schedule an email slot might feel ridiculous or constricting. It might sound odd to say *Try some cooking* when it's your work day that is intense. I don't know your struggles. Some of these things might have a dramatic effect. Some might feel like sticking plasters. A lot of that is down to how much control you have over the intensity of your day. The elephant in the room when it comes to such intensity is workload. If there is too much to do, the job will be intense and potentially overwhelming. In Part 4, we'll examine how to reduce workload, not just manage it.

Key Takeaways

- Intensity at work can be defined as 'the rate of physical and/or mental input to work tasks performed during the working day.'

- Work intensity seems to be more of an issue for teachers than those in many other professions.

- Teachers are bombarded with information, tasks, and distractions throughout the working day. The more of these we receive, the more intense our day becomes.

- The negative effects of such intensity include fatigue, stress, poorer job performance, and reduced job satisfaction.

Whilst we can feel that the intensity of our day is out of our control, there are things we can do to manage it.

● Plan *where* you work to minimise distraction.

● Plan *when* you work to prioritise more complex tasks for distraction-free times. Schedule more difficult work, like planning for a new topic, in periods in the day when you know you have the time and space to complete it.

● Take breaks at work. You work better after a break, and you feel better after connecting with colleagues (ok, *most* colleagues).

● Leave as much work as possible at work and plan to minimise any work you have to do at home.

● Schedule enriching activities outside of work. You're likely to feel better about work if you return from activities where you experience a sense of mastery or connection.

Notes

1 Green, F. (2021). British teachers' declining job quality: Evidence from the skills and employment survey. *Oxford Review of Education*, 47(3), 386–403.
2 For excellent advice in this area, I'd recommend Tom Bennett's *Running the Room*.
3 Romano, S., Scanniello, G., Fucci, D., Juristo, N., and Turhan, B. (2017). The effect of noise on software engineers' performance. In Proceedings of the 12th ACM/IEEE International Symposium on Empirical Software Engineering and Measurement (ESEM '18). Association for Computing Machinery, New York, NY, USA, Article 9, 1–10. .
4 Kaplan, S. (1995). The restorative benefits of nature: Toward and integrative framework. *Journal of Environmental Psychology*, 16, 169–182.
5 Willingham, D. (2017). Irrelevant interruptions and their cost to thinking. Accessed from http://www.danielwillingham.com/daniel-willingham-science-and-education-blog/irrelevant-interruptions-and-their-cost-to-thinking (accessed on 20/3/2023).
6 Archsmith, J., Heyes, A., Neidell, M., and Sampat, B. (2021). The dynamics of inattention in the (baseball) field. Institute of Labour Economics Discussion Paper Series.
7 Danziger, S., Levav, J., and Avnaim-Pesso, L. (2011). Extraneous factors in judicial decisions. *PNAS*, 108(17), 6889–6892.
8 Kern, M. L., Waters, L., Adler, A., and White, M. (2014). Assessing employee wellbeing in schools using a multifaceted approach: Associations with physical health, life satisfaction, and professional thriving. *Psychology*, 5, 500–513.
9 Van Hooff, M. L. M., Flaxman, P. E., Söderberg, M., Stride, C. B., and Geurts, S. A. E. (2018). Basic psychological need satisfaction, recovery state, and recovery timing. *Human Performance*, 31(2), 125–143.
10 Newport, C. (2016). *Deep Work*. London: Piatakus.
11 Kaplan, S. The restorative benefits of nature: Toward and integrative framework.
12 Kaplan, S., and Berman, M. (2010). Directed attention as a common resource for executive functioning and self-regulation. *Perspectives on Psychological Science*, 5(1), 43–57.
13 Oppezzo, M., and Schwartz, D. (2014). Give your ideas some legs: The positive effect of walking on creative thinking. *American Psychological Association*, 40(4), 1142–1152.
14 Santelli, F., and Grissom, J. (2022). A bad commute: Does travel time to work predict teacher and leader turnover and other workplace outcomes? (EdWorkingPaper: 22-691).

15 Pindek, S., Shen, W., and Andel, S. (2022). Finally, some "me time": A new theoretical perspective on the benefits of commuting. *Organizational Psychology Review*, 13(1), 44–66.

16 Martin, A., Gorykakin, Y., and Suhrcke, M. (2014). Does active commuting improve psychological wellbeing? Longitudinal evidence from eighteen waves of the British Household Panel Survey. *Preventative Medicine*, 69, 296–303.

17 Martin, A., Gorykakin, Y., and Suhrcke, M. Does active commuting improve psychological wellbeing? Longitudinal evidence from eighteen waves of the British Household Panel Survey.

18 Pindek, S., Shen, W., and Andel, S. Finally, some "me time": A new theoretical perspective on the benefits of commuting.

⚓ Managing Intensity – Notes for Leaders

You have the power to make a colleague's day more or less intense. This power shouldn't be taken lightly. We should be mindful of the effect an email we send, a conversation we have, a meeting we lead can have on our colleagues. Use the points below to spark a conversation with your leadership team. Use these questions to help you:

● Which practices do we need to stop?

● What do we need to refine or change?

● What do we need to communicate or model to staff?

Stop trying to get people to work harder. As work intensity expert Professor Francis Green points out, 'getting people to work harder is inherently self-limiting as a growth strategy, unlike investing in their human capabilities.'[1] Of course, leaders want staff to 'work hard,' but it's an unhelpful lie to think you can always eke out a little bit more from staff. Decisions made by leaders, initiatives introduced, policies planned – all must weigh up what they are adding not just to the workload of staff but to the intensity of each day. Sure, we could push staff by adding an extra duty to their timetable, but if we don't have to, keeping this time free for them will reap the refreshing benefits of breaks. We could mandate a same-day call home policy for missed homework, but to what extent will that create an unmanageable expectation on staff? Ask yourself (and your leadership team):

● How will this policy/initiative/request add to or alter the day of a teacher with a full timetable?

● Is there any way we can reduce expectations of staff elsewhere in order to make this change?

● Have we asked what staff think of this proposal?

DOI: 10.4324/9781003453154-11

Make information flow your priority. One driver of intensity is the quantity of incoming information, tasks, and requests. Not only that, failure to manage this information well – poor communication or bureaucratic processes – is likely drive up stress in your staff. And this stress is likely to spread, making an organisation feel stressful.[2]

If, each day, staff have new items from different sources added to their to-do lists, feelings that the job is relentless will spike. It's likely that no one will have much of a handle on how much is being expected of staff in a given day, week, or term. Two things to try:

- **Briefings and bulletins**. To my shame and pride, I once was part of a covert Briefing Bingo group in a school that had a daily briefing. We'd take it in turns to write down likely briefing events and awarded each other with chocolate when someone filled their card. We were gently mocking a process that often felt unnecessary, where emails were repeated (at times, verbatim), and, on occasion, there were no messages at all. In-person briefings, or bulletins, can work where they bring all information together for staff in one place. If heads of year, Duke of Edinburgh coordinators, mental health leads, SENCOs (special educational needs coordinators), and everyone in between know that messages *must* be relayed to staff through a particular channel, then we minimise the quantity coming out to everyone separately.

  Email inflation occurs where you receive so many irrelevant messages that you start to ignore *all* messages. A briefing or bulletin (or both) can serve to eliminate that kind of inflation as long as the process is used by all, and staff who don't use it – including leaders – are corrected quickly.

- **Coordinating messages**. When campaigning, political parties might have a 'message calendar', an organised schedule of when certain topics are going to be front and centre. Too often in schools, leaders are competing for their messages to get through to staff. One leader wants to make homework a priority, another is entirely focused on contact with home. In some schools, line managers of phases or year teams or subject areas coordinate their messages, but this does nothing to alleviate intensity if there isn't some work being done to prioritise. Priority means *of first importance*. It's not possible to have 12 priorities, although schools often try.

  Leaders should meet at the start of a term to define the key dates, deadlines, and *priorities* for staff. Regular meetings should set the direction for line management of middle leaders and others. These meetings should remind leaders of current priorities and how to focus on those with line-managed areas. Standing questions on the agenda of these meetings should be

- How can we keep focused on this priority (and avoid other important distractions)?

- What are we delaying, cutting, or not expecting whilst we focus on *this* priority?

- How will our message to staff change in the coming weeks or terms?

Put a limit on email. Leaders should model good email practice. Not sending an email for every little thing. Never *replying all* (ever). But leaders should also be clear on the email culture we're trying to create. Email breeds email. If we send fewer emails, we'll likely receive fewer.

Minimise meeting intensity. It can feel satisfying to get all the messages we need to communicate out in one meeting. Once those messages are out there in the atmosphere, staff are accountable for any actions associated. There's a *They've heard it so they should be doing it* philosophy that can creep into leader planning of a meeting cycle. There's a logic to this approach but a faulty logic. Too often these messages and meetings, even training, are planned entirely from the perspective of someone who spends more time in their office than they do teaching. Understanding how staff experience training and meetings is vital if we want to sequence a set of messages in a way that will genuinely be illuminating and supportive.

Expect staff to have a break. Teachers will be more likely to teach, plan, and do everything else effectively if they have had a break during the day. A lack of breaks is likely to lead to lower-quality work and poorer decisions. So scheduling meetings or expecting extra curricula activities in break or lunch time with zero discussion about how that will affect staff is a self-defeating act. It is not that these things can *never* happen. It is that we should think carefully about how they are implemented. Is a member of staff who runs a club given a payback in the duties expected of them? Or are they able to decide when it runs so they can place it on a lighter day? Even jokes about staff 'slacking' because they are taking lunch with colleagues create an atmosphere where having a break is discouraged.

Have zero expectation about how long staff stay at school. Staff should be allowed and, more importantly, encouraged to work in a way that works for them. Where other jobs have experienced increasing flexibility in recent years, schools understandably can't offer the kind of flexible working found elsewhere. Instead, we should maximise the flexibility available to us. Apart from being on time to school, we should expect nothing from staff in terms of how early they are in and how late they leave. More than that, leaders should model, wherever possible, how flexible the job can be. Making a comment about leaving early to meet a friend, saying you can't attend a late meeting because you're taking your daughter swimming, saying you're going to leave promptly and will give an email some thought later – all of these create an atmosphere where leaving whenever you want is acceptable. Any school still instituting bizarre rules about the work day – *You must be here until five* – should be ashamed and change them quickly. Of course, there will be expectations of staff – meetings, parents' evenings, completing the duties of a teacher – but if the standard is met, we shouldn't care when a teacher leaves school.

If working until 6 every evening so a teacher doesn't have to take work home is the way they want to work, fine. But leaders and line managers should check in regularly with those who do work long and late to make sure they are supported.

A dangerous flipside to having no expectation of when staff arrive or leave is the expectation that staff are *always on*. Just as there should be no expectation of staff being at school beyond the school day and scheduled meetings, we shouldn't expect staff to respond to emails out of hours or at the weekend. Messages to staff that expect immediate/by-tomorrow/over-the-weekend responses or action create a culture of constant work. Leaders should never send an email in an evening or a weekend asking for a 'chat' with a colleague the following day or week. It causes unnecessary stress; just go and talk to people!

Notes

1 Green, F., Felstead, A., and Henseke, G. (2022). Working still harder. *LR Review*, 75(2), 458–487.
2 Altindag, O. (2020). Relationship between stress management and job performance in organizations. *Research in Business and Social Science (2147–4478)*, 9(2), 43–49.

PART 3
Embedding Habits

Problem	Solution
Chapter 7 We can't force ourselves into behaviours that are more effective.	Develop a practice habit.
Chapter 8 Over time, we embed subpar habits.	Replace existing habits with ones that are more effective.

DOI: 10.4324/9781003453154-12

7 Practice

Problem	Solution
We can't force ourselves into behaviours that are more effective.	Develop a practice habit.

Rachael has been teaching for three years, and she does not like Year 9.

Every Year 9 lesson approaches like those drops on the rollercoaster, the ones where you've slowly ratcheted towards an upward horizon. The gradual, almost gentle, tilt. The view of the drop before the terrifying descent.

In this way, Year 9 lessons sort of pass Rachael by. She stands at the front and tells the students to do things. They don't do them. Or some do but lots don't. And the ones who don't are the loudest.

A half-term ends and Rachael looks back. She wanted to change but somehow didn't manage to. She thought about getting someone in to look at her seating plan or going back to the behaviour policy with an experienced colleague. Or planning simpler lessons that didn't require her to split her attention so much between different bits of the task and different groups of students.

A desire to change has not resulted in changed behaviour. What's going wrong?

Problem

That teaching is busy and varied hardly needs stating. In fact, these are some of the things that make teaching enjoyable and rewarding. An exciting but full day is more satisfying than a predictable, empty one. Here, though, we find one of the core challenges of being a teacher. Large quantities of new information hurtle towards you from moment to moment. Ideas, tasks, questions, and processes in the hundreds, if not thousands, pass through the teacher's mind each day, but this is only the start of the problem.

DOI: 10.4324/9781003453154-13

In this chapter, we'll examine how we can change and improve our behaviours and actions through practice, repetition, and refinement of optimal processes. In the next, we'll turn our attention to prompts and cues that can nudge our habitual behaviour towards a desired state.

The limits and potential of human cognitive architecture

Universal limitations of the human mind have particular consequences for teachers and teaching. To understand these consequences, we need to understand a theory with implications for teaching but also our development as teachers: cognitive load theory.

The willpower problem

Every one of us is limited and constrained by our working memory. Working memory or conscious thought, what we're thinking of in any given moment, can hold within it only a small number of new items at once.[1] Like a juggler adding ball after ball, we find that at a certain point our attention, our minds, can't cope. We can't focus. We don't remember each new thing. We underperform. Teachers instinctively know this. Experience evidences it: teaching out of specialism and struggling to manage behaviour; teaching a new class and struggling to pitch an explanation; trying to plan and resource for a new topic and struggling to make progress; teaching in a new phase or school and feeling like you're back at square one.

If working memory is so creaky under pressure, how can the human mind perform feats of creativity, problem-solving, and deep thought? How can a teacher achieve anything when the quantities of new information assaulting the structures of our mind during lesson time are so high? The answer is long-term memory. Knowledge and processes embedded in long-term memory can be accessed without putting the same strain on our working memory. We can explain more effectively, managing behaviour as we go, when the content we explain is embedded in long-term memory. We can run more fluid, purposeful class discussion when names are embedded in long-term memory.

Automation of knowledge and process makes our lives easier. But how do we get there? Wanting a change doesn't seem to cut it. To use a fancy term, habits aren't *goal-dependent*. We can deeply desire a certain behaviour. We can aim for change of some kind. We can want to improve. Yet those goals can struggle to assert themselves over our habitual behaviour. As behavioural science researchers point out, 'failures of self-control often persist even when people recognize them and resolve to act differently in the future.'[2]

Where willpower fails, automation can succeed because it doesn't require us to white-knuckle through tiredness, distraction, or a lack of motivation. All of us in every domain of life automate processes. We put a seatbelt on before we start the car. We turn the kettle on when we walk into the kitchen. We check our phones in empty moments even when we don't need or want to. The same is true in our classrooms. Phrases the children could quote back to us, the ones we use each and every lesson, go unnoticed by us. Quirks in mannerism and gesture hilarious to our classes are almost invisible to us.

We would not survive, in life or the classroom, if we didn't embed some automatic processes. There is simply too much to think about and do. This chapter and this section focus on intentionally developing effective automated habits and breaking bad habits that have developed unintentionally.

Best worst days

I could probably quote, as well as a few choice lines of Shakespeare, large chunks of dialogue from *The West Wing* on demand. In the show, Jed Bartlet, idealistic, knowledgeable President of the United States, battles for progress against the forces that get in the way, including his own demons.

In one episode, Bartlet is trying to appoint a new Chief Justice to the Supreme Court. He wants to replace an aging member of the court with someone young and effective. But, because of the gridlocked legislative system, Bartlet can't appoint who he would like. He could offer up a substandard compromise candidate and this is what he tries to do. The aging judge pushes back saying, 'On my worst days, I am better than the amped-up ambulance chasers you could get confirmed.' Even though the judge's mind and memory are fading, he recognises that at a base level, he's better than most. There's a standard he doesn't drop below.

Some quotations inhabit a corner of our minds, speaking to us long after they've been ripped from their context. I often turn this particular quotation over in my mind, wondering what standard I drop to on my worst days. Universal to all teachers is a concern about being present but distracted, about the quality we've achieved and the quality we'd *like* to achieve. We turn up to work ill because setting cover is more hassle than we want. We turn up after stressful family mornings, depositing our own children at nursery or before-school club and then attending to other people's. We know there's a peak we reach, maybe just occasionally, that we want more of.

Unfortunately, achievement does not come from simply wanting it more. Without a system for a teacher, a set of behaviours and methods of changing behaviours, we won't be able to rise to and maintain the level we're after.

If we recognise that automation of behaviour is going to happen – it doesn't simply happen to some of us – then we need to recognise that our success and failure as an effective teacher depend on how well we've automated key behaviours. The quality of those best worst days is decided before they begin.

Solutions

James has been teaching Geography for ten years. His relaxed style is what he feels endears him to his students. And, to an extent, he's right. Students like James. They joke with him. They chat to him on duty. They do enjoy his lessons, although some students feel they get away with too much.

James has been asked by his head of department to use the language set out in the behaviour policy to raise his expectations of how students should behave in his lessons. It's been made clear that this is about both reducing negative behaviour, such as off-task chat, calling out, and rudeness, and promoting positive behaviours, such as effort, self-regulation, and enthusiasm for the subject. The head of department has suggested that James script and practise certain phrases in order to automate them so that they can be used readily. James's reluctance to do this stems from his feeling that this would change his lessons and, more than that, who he is as a teacher.

Before we get to the methods of automation, to how James might change this behaviour, we need to understand more about how it works. Psychology professor and expert on teacher development David Feldon describes the qualities of automaticity. An automated act

- 'Occurs without intention.'

- 'Is not subject to conscious monitoring.'

- 'Utilizes few, if any, attentional resources.'

- 'Happens rapidly.'[3]

Notice how these align with aspects of teaching and cut against the grain of others. Teaching feels like an intentional act. A lesson we're teaching, particularly with *that* class, needs conscious monitoring; children in front of us need our attention. How do we square all that with this call to automate?

To be the *caring* teacher who has time for their students, we might need to make sure the behaviour management processes are so strong for our class that we are able to talk to the one student who needs us at the start of the lesson. If we want to be the teacher who *knows their stuff*, who can talk about subject content easily, we need to automate aspects of our teaching, from explanation to check for understanding. If we want to be the teacher who *gets lots done*, or works the students hard, we need strong classroom routines.

James, our geography teacher, couldn't really see the point of reaching automaticity until his head of department talked about it making his life easier and making him better at his job whilst expending less effort. It wasn't about turning him into an entirely different person or an entirely different teacher. When they first talked about embedding some new habits, James was also worried that every moment of his lessons was going to be controlled or directed. In fact, the language suggested to James will be used in a small fraction of the time in his lessons but could make a massive difference.

You can automate anything but not everything

Automated actions are one of the levers we pull to change our behaviour.

This can happen in two main ways:

- **We automate processes that achieve our goals**. We want to be a good explainer, so we script and rehearse. Our goal is the smooth running of lessons, so we define and practise the routines likely to support calm transitions through the lessons.

- **We automate processes that free up time and mental space to achieve our goals**. We organise resources and our rooms to save time, so we can leave earlier, achieving our goal of seeing more of our family.

Of course, you don't have complete control over what needs to be automatic and what doesn't. We can talk about two broad categories:

- **Behaviours directed by your school**. Some schools designate a set of behaviours that everyone *must* do. In the best cases, these behaviours are part of a collective effort to improve behaviour or maximise lesson time. A secondary school might mandate that every teacher meet students in the corridor at the start of every lesson.

- **Behaviours selected by you**. More important than those behaviours you are asked to automate are the behaviours you decide to automate yourself. A gap exists between your current state and the desired state. Desire, on its own, counts for less than we'd expect. Choosing behaviours to refine and automate will shape our development like a funnel directing what is forced through it. If we fall to the level of our systems, it's our responsibility to design systems that make us into more effective teachers.

Finally, there are two realms in which we can automate behaviour:

- **In the classroom**. Our actions create routines, make subject knowledge clear, and elicit student participation. If, each time we teach, we're uncertain about these actions, we leave learning – and our effectiveness as a teacher – to chance. If we plan out how we'll behave, if we create a system to ensure we behave in this way, we make it more likely, despite the distractions of the day, that we'll teach well.

- **Outside the classroom.** To make best use of our time and ensure we spend time on the *right things*, we don't just automate habits in the classroom. What we do when we arrive at school or before we leave or how we start PPA (planning, preparation, and assessment) and how we manage and respond to email are routines that can be automated.

We do this to get to the substance of our goals. Too often, we plan to work on our goals but the quantity of work or intensity of teaching means we look back at a day uncomfortably aware of the lack of progress.

See automation differently

In this chapter, more than any other, the solution is tightly tied to the problem. We need to reach automaticity of certain behaviours and challenge the automaticity of others. We're going to zoom in on practice as a lever for quickly attaining automated and effective behaviour.

To do that, in the rest of this chapter we'll

- Build awareness of effective behaviours

- Define the behaviours that will serve our goals

- Understand how practice can embed these behaviours

- Put this in the context of how we are developing

Build awareness

We don't know what we don't know. So much of what might be possible to change exists beyond the periphery of our awareness. For every area where we feel clear about possible next steps, four or five probably exist where we just aren't sure.

It's our job as teachers looking to improve and sustain effective careers to be outward-looking. This is not the frenzied search for the next and the new. It is the careful curation of the useful and applicable, real solutions to genuine problems we're facing.

We're looking for

- Strategies and approaches in the classroom.

- Ways of working as a teacher (including planning, feeding back, and time management)

We can look for these things

● In our school

● Beyond our school

● In writing and other resources

We can do this by

● Reading

● Observing colleagues

● Visiting schools

● Joining and making networks

● Seeking out models of effective teaching

● Sharing our experiences with colleagues

Define the behaviours that serve your goals

A goal is an ambitious sense of direction. It is the way you're pointing and the place you want to get to. It is the person you are becoming, a better version of you. But, on its own, without something actionable, a goal will remain an alternate reality of what might have been. If you need to, return to Chapter 4 to revisit setting meaningful goals.

To have a goal, you don't have to have every step on that journey figured out. But it should be clear to you what behaviour will need to be introduced, changed, or removed.

You could draw a table like the one below and use it to plan change deliberately and consider first steps.

My Goals	First Steps
Improve the atmosphere and behaviour in my classroom by pre-empting poor behaviour.	Get books and resources ready before the lesson Make sure I stand at the door to meet most difficult classes.
Manage my time, particularly PPA time, more effectively.	Schedule specific activities for my PPA and before school.

Don't worry too much about *Which first step should go first?* There probably won't be a *right* answer to that question. Instead, we're going to sort those behaviours into two categories: things we can practice and things we can't.

Choosing what and how to practice

Expert teachers aren't the sum of their automated behaviours. Teaching itself, we know, isn't simply about how we act. We aren't the gymnast, perfectly executing a routine that has been broken down, practised, put back together before a competition, all without the audience or judges present.

The complexity of the classroom means that this kind of practice will only ever be partial. Classroom behaviours are the tip of the iceberg resting on a mass of subject knowledge, knowledge of students, of learning and much more.[4]

At times, a behaviour doesn't feel practicable. Perhaps it's an out-of-lesson behaviour. You want to arrive at school and check through your to-do list or planning before checking email. Simply sitting at your desk for extended periods and intending not checking your email is unlikely to change that behaviour. Chapter 8 will focus on how to nudge our behaviour in the right direction when practice doesn't feel like the right tool.

Practice deliberately

That said, the power of practice is well documented.

Anders Ericsson defines the qualities of *deliberate practice* as

- Activity outside of a person's comfort zone.
- Focus on a narrow behaviour within a domain.
- Practice of that narrow behaviour in isolation.
- Feedback to improve the behaviour.
- Refinement of the behaviour as it is repeated.[5]

Rehearsal and role-play are more likely to induce a cringe than a smile. *You want me to act? To pretend like I'm talking to the children when I'm not?* To overcome the cringe, we can do a couple of things.

First, we can see practice on a spectrum from **Good Intentions** through to **Deliberate Practice**. When we really want to change something we do in the classroom, that change becomes more likely the further we push ourselves along this spectrum.

Good intentions		Purposeful practice		Deliberate practice
A desire to change	Individual practice (e.g. in the car on the way to work)	Scripting, individual practice, iteration	Filming or recording with iteration	Defined behaviour, rehearsal, feedback, iteration

Deliberate practice, according to Ericsson, involves isolating the behaviour, practising it, and refining it after feedback. If you're ready to start there, that's great, but you might not be able to, particularly if you don't have someone to give you feedback.

That doesn't mean you can't practise if you're on your own. And, if you don't want to jump straight to deliberate practice, experiment with some of the elements of it.

You've already, hopefully, defined some behaviours you want to embed. See those behaviours, for a moment, through the lens of the following options.

- *Go for it.* If you're just getting into practice and you know what you want to change, you can practise that thing by yourself. Perhaps you want to be quicker to give warnings in your classroom without getting into a back-and-forth about the injustices of the behaviour system.

    Play around with phrases – *Jon, that's a warning. You're talking... Jon, warning for talking.* Benefits of this approach include the ability to do it in the car, whilst you're having breakfast or getting your classroom set up for the day. But real limitations exist at this level, too: you won't receive feedback, so you might miss something or embed a subpar behaviour. Perhaps the biggest limitation of this approach is our tendency to *intend* to do it rather than actually do it. We run through warnings in our head, but they don't crystalise because we haven't really practised. We've just *thought about* practising.

- *Script it.* Whilst *Going for it* can work in some circumstances, the intentional act of scripting forces us to consider more thoroughly what it is we want to practise. We script something when fidelity to a success criterion or model is important. In fact, before we script for practice, benefits can be reaped from models of that successful behaviour. Watching models of a teaching behaviour is more likely to improve that behaviour than simply reading about a certain technique.[6]

    Scripting reminds us that there is a standard we're trying to reach (or not drop below). A script might include the key words or analogies you want to use in an explanation or the format with which you want to ask a question. A script might be on a Post-it note, on our resources, or on a screen in front of us.

    Crucially, a script might be useful if we haven't practised (where we use it like an aide-memoire in our lessons) or haven't practised much, but it's likely to be more useful when we've practised with it first. That way, we prepare to meet the standard aimed for and make it more likely we'll reach it.

- *Plan it.* Here, we do more than just *intend*; we build a behaviour into our planning. If a check for understanding is missing from our day-to-day teaching, we set aside time to plan a check into our lessons. It's on a PowerPoint slide or we prepare to check by setting out the mini-whiteboards before the lesson. Engineer a situation in which practice is more likely.

● **Record it.** Where practice with another human isn't possible, practising with a device that will record what you're doing can be invaluable. A recording offers us something we can't do for ourselves: the opportunity to detach and actually listen to or watch what we're doing. Particularly if you want to get a phrasing right, perhaps when giving quick feedback on misconceptions, recording and refining can work really well. Recordings can be made outside of lessons as you practise a behaviour in isolation, but we can also record and return to a behaviour as we try to embed it into a lesson.

● **Practise it, deliberately.** In some schools, the Continuing Professional Development model will weave in opportunities for a kind of practice. Perhaps there's a frequent meeting where staff practise common behaviours or a coaching model includes practice within it. Without these things, it can be difficult to get to *deliberate* practice on your own; you'll need, at least, to invite someone you trust and respect to watch you practise and support you with feedback.

When I asked several of the teachers I interviewed, most of them were clear that they hadn't engaged in much more than the *Go for it* model of practice: trying ideas out and seeing if they work. Some had positive experiences of practice; others didn't. Looking back on our progress, we can engage in a kind of survivorship bias where because we've made it this far without practice, we think it won't help us solve current problems.

Here are some examples of how we might use the ideas above:

Behaviour is difficult in the transitions between activities	*Script it* by writing out specific phrases you intend to use. *Record* your use of these phrases or, if you can, practise *deliberately* with a colleague before the lesson and get them to observe your use of them during the lesson.
The class have embedded a misconception about a topic	*Script* your explanation and make sure your *plan* prompts you to explain in a way that tackles this misconception. *Record* it and listen back to check it covers what you wanted in the clearest possible way.
Some students regularly struggle to start independent work and don't have a clear idea of what success looks like	*Plan* your model so that you can do it effortlessly under the visualiser. Check your plan with a colleague.
Despite asking hands-down questions, lessons often seem to leave some students behind	*Plan* specific checks for the whole class, perhaps using mini-whiteboards. *Script* your introduction to the task and questions so it's clear for students.

Receive feedback

Moving between the options above as seems appropriate is fine. Don't feel bad if you can't get all the way down the spectrum to deliberate practice. Just try to push yourself further in that direction where you can.

Practice will only be as useful as the way it helps us to refine our behaviour. Rarely do we start out practising the perfect version of a behaviour, easily dropping it into our already near-perfect teaching practice. Feedback's vital role is to refine a behaviour both as we practise it but also as we try to embed it into the classroom.

Feedback takes various shapes depending on the type of practice and the resources available.

On our own

At times, we're not able to receive feedback from a person, so we can engineer, perhaps imperfect, methods of giving ourselves feedback. Here, you might feel like I'm stretching the definition of feedback, but, to my mind, feedback is any information that helps us to refine the practice we're trying to implement.

We can *give ourselves feedback* by

a. Defining success criteria

b. Practising with and against these criteria

c. Checking we've met the success criteria

Various pitfalls mean we could *think* we're spending time in this area when we're actually existing in a hollowed out version of it. Those pitfalls would include

● Success criteria that don't exactly define what we need to do to improve.

● No clear check that success criteria are met.

We can avoid these pitfalls by

● Sourcing our success criteria from something, someone, or somewhere other than ourselves.

● Recording our implementation of the success criteria.

The combination of a success criterion and recording can be a powerful one. If we know *wait time* is the goal, listening back to questions and the pauses after them can be a powerfully direct way of checking if the habit is taking. Safety instructions in Design Technology will have to include certain important specifics; recording the practice of these instructions in the classroom by ourselves before checking we've covered the essentials is more likely to embed the behaviour than good intentions.

It's impossible to do this for *every* strategy or technique that make up our teaching practice. Selection of behaviours must be done carefully, underpinned by the questions *What problem am I trying to solve? What am I trying to make easier for myself?* If the processes above feel unnecessary or overwrought, it may be that, for certain behaviours, they are. Leave this process for when you want to change and can devote some time to it.

From others

As you can see, feedback is easier when we have another pair of eyes. Deliberate practice, as described by Ericsson, is intended for the audience of the coach or feedback giver.

When receiving feedback from another, it can feel like the power is theirs and theirs alone. *They* will tell *you* what to do or what you got right and wrong. Whilst there are times when this is the case because you may miss things that they have seen, the feedback is there to change *your* behaviour so *you* are in control of what it achieves and how effective it is.

Remember:

- **For feedback to effectively change behaviour, it should** focus on the focus. There should be a very good reason to give feedback on something *other than what you're practising.* If someone gives you feedback on something other than the practised area, bring them back to it. If the feedback feels important, you could ask, *We're working on X. Do you think Y is more important?* And switch to practising something else

- **The narrower the feedback, the easier it is to action**. Feedback should result in a step or steps for you to take. If you're practising an explanation and a coach asks you to 'be clearer' or if you aren't getting either confirmation that you're on the right track or a clear alteration to make, the feedback probably isn't going to help. Prompt a focus on by asking the feedback giver, *What should I change? How should I translate what you've said into what I'm doing?* The danger here is superficial response to feedback that is looking for an easy, but not necessarily the most important, lever to pull. Also ask, *Is this going to make an important difference to what I'm doing? What will the impact on the children be?*

Return to what this feedback is *for*. Our concern is with solving the problems and the challenges that persistently confront teachers. Any behaviour you're trying to embed is meant to be making you a more effective teacher more of the time. It should also make your life easier in some way.

It's easier to have

● One routine for moving from carpet to tables than to make one up each time.

● One routine for feedback as you circulate rather than do different things each time.

● Clear structures for class discussion so you don't have to remind classes of rules they can't remember.

● Routines for handing out resources, taking them back in, packing up, leaving the room, and a lot more.

It's also like you're a more effective teacher as you do all these things: behaviour is better, time isn't wasted, and learning is richer.

If feedback doesn't help to make your life easier or confuses you or implementing it gives you considerably more work than is feasible, it's not helpful feedback for our purpose. Feedback can feel uncomfortable; at times, it might hurt because we care about how we're doing. But it should help.

Iterate

Behaviours aren't mastered in one session by yourself in your classroom or in one coaching conversation. When we put deliberate practice on a pedestal, we forget that we're practising all day, every day. Classroom behaviour is so hard to change because so much of it is happening each day. Frequent, short practice sessions can have an impact, but the focus must be narrow, and we must return to what we're trying to refine.

Practice meets reality as a reminder, sometimes a painful one, that teaching isn't just a set of practicable behaviours that we can perfect outside the classroom. An explanation, crafted with care and attention, can be swept away by a tide of misconceptions or poor behaviour. A behaviour script to deal with low-level behaviour can be knocked off course by *that* student's bad day.

After practising a behaviour outside of a lesson (or during), ask yourself

● Did that go as I expected?

● Did I have to change what I practised?

● Did it have the impact I wanted or expected?

● How should I refine this further?

Confirmation bias can creep into these answers when we want to see improvement. Tie your answer to the evidence in your behaviour and the change in your classroom. Of course, you can ask yourself these questions with a tool like video or audio recording, or a coach can help you through them.

Remember in all of this our aim is to make ourselves more effective more of the time. At times, a feeling of *I worked really hard and that didn't get me anywhere* can follow a period of practice. Many teachers, quite understandably, don't feel they have the time to go through the processes above, particularly when they aren't mandated, when time is not set aside for them, by schools and leaders. Practice, especially practice we self-direct, is an investment. As in all investments, care should be taken about what we're devoting resources to. But not to invest anything, anywhere, will likely lead to disappointment and discouragement.

Look for what practice achieves

A teacher with an easier life is less overwhelmed by the intensity of the job, by the onslaught of information. But, perhaps more importantly, to improve, we need to have the mental space to *notice* things, things we could notice because *some* of our practice has been automated. We need the mental space that allows us to think and reflect and plan. As our experience in a domain grows, and with that experience a set of automated behaviours, we start to focus on the more complex aspects within the domain.[7] Complex problems come to be seen as simpler, and attention, freed from prior constraint, is 're-allocated'[8] to new problems we'd only just realised existed.

What, then, do you need automation for? There are times when change is essential. To improve. To move with our school or team. To make life easier. It would be reasonable to ask, *Easier for what?*

We could view our development as a ladder we're training ourselves to climb. This ladder is massive; it stretches far beyond the limits of our eyesight. Initially, we're only strong enough to pull ourselves up onto the first few rungs. Burgeoning knowledge and automated processes increase our strength to get a little bit higher.

To stretch the metaphor too far, we can remain at the bottom of the ladder even if we have the strength to go higher. Strength won through automation of process will see returns diminishing unless we look to the next rung on that ladder. We need to apply the knowledge we're developing to the next challenge in the classroom.[9] Some examples:

- An entry routine through to first task has been automated. Students come in, hand out books, and get on with the first task. Now, it's possible to circulate a quiet classroom, assessing what students have got and what they haven't and challenging them where they don't get started quickly.

- Modelling under the visualiser is no longer a challenge. Not quite effortless but not far off. this is down to careful planning: notes go on the left-hand page of the exercise book, the model goes on the right. It's also down to practice during and outside of the lesson. Now, the pauses during the model become opportunities for questions, checks, and student thinking. This takes more planning and fresh mental effort.

● Perhaps it was wrong to see it as *taming* behaviour, but that's how it felt. Clear boundaries clearly communicated. Warnings practised in an empty classroom until automatic. Then delivered with precise, detached language. Some students were sent out, but they came back clearer on expectation. More of the class are calmer more of the time. Now, it's possible to work more closely with those causing more of the difficulties, to give them time to make the right choice, to develop relationships derived from more than warnings and consequences.

Consider where your next rungs are by answering the following questions:

● What have you mastered that was difficult previously?

● What is automatic that used to be effortful?

● What problems present themselves that you didn't notice before?

● Where would you like to direct your energies next?

We said the first angle from which to view automating processes was the way it increases our mental capacity.

The second is how we embed more effective practices more of the time. When we consider the questions above, the problem of what's effective and what isn't becomes all the more important.

Practice isn't the only way we change our behaviour. Our next chapter looks at all the ways we can nudge our behaviour when practice might not be the right tool.

Key Takeaways

● Willpower alone won't lead to change. Surprisingly, just *wanting* to change something doesn't necessarily lead to change.

● Deliberate practice is the isolated practice of a narrow behaviour, followed by specific feedback and iteration.

● Practice should serve our goals. We should practise the behaviours that we at least believe will help us to achieve the outcomes we're working towards.

● Teachers can practise on a spectrum from good intentions – *I'd like to change X* – through to deliberate practice. In between, we might script a new behaviour or film ourselves and check our behaviour against a success criterion. The needs of the moment often get in the way of deliberate practice, but that doesn't mean our practice – whatever the format – is worthless.

● Practice should win us more space in our mental capacity to develop further. If we've practised a behaviour until it is automatic, we don't need to think about that behaviour in the same way anymore.

Notes

1 Estimates put this number somewhere between four and seven.
2 Duckworth, A., Milkman, K., and Laibson, D. (2018). Beyond willpower: Strategies for reducing failures of self-control. *Psychological Science in the Public Interest*, 19(3), 102–129.
3 Feldon, D. (2007). Cognitive load and classroom teaching: The double-edged sword of automaticity. *Educational Psychologist*, 42(3), 123–137.
4 For more on the knowledge teachers need to develop expertise, see my first book, *What Do New Teachers Need to Know?*
5 See, for example, Ericsson, A., Krampe, R., and Tesch Romer, K. (1993). The role of deliberate practice in the acquisition of expert performance. *Psychological Review*, 100(3), 363–406. Ericsson, A. (2006); The influence of experience and deliberate practice on the development of superior expert performance. In Ericsson, A. (Ed.), *The Cambridge Handbook of Expertise and Expert Performance*. Cambridge, Cambridge University Press, pp. 683–704; Ericsson, A. (2008). Deliberate practice and acquisition of expert performance: A general overview. *Academic Emergency Medicine*, 15, 988–994.
6 Sims, S., Fletcher-Wood, H., O'Mara-Eves, A., Cottingham, S., Stansfield, C., Van Herwegen, J., and Anders, J. (2021). *What are the Characteristics of Teacher Professional Development that Increase Pupil Achievement? A Systematic Review and Meta-Analysis*. London: Education Endowment Foundation.
7 Allegra Forest, T., Siegelman, N., and Finn, A. (2022). Attention shifts to more complex structures with experience. *Psychological Science*, 33(12), 2059–2072.
8 Allegra Forest, T., Siegelman, N., and Finn, A. Attention shifts to more complex structures with experience.
9 For more of a discussion about how this kind of expertise develops, see Bereiter, C., and Scardamalia, M. (1993). *Surpassing Ourselves*. Chicago, Open Court Publishing.

8 Habit

Problem	Solution
Over time, we embed subpar habits.	Replace existing habits with ones that are more effective.

Mel is a reluctant convert to routine. As we talk about the classroom routines she has set up, Mel tells me, 'This is not my natural way of being at all.' Like many teachers, Mel starts her day early. 'I tend to get into school by half-seven, sometimes earlier.' What happens next is pretty much the same each day:

> I log on to the computer, get my starters loaded and anything else open I need like YouTube videos or whatever. Then I check any emails that can be dealt with quickly and if I can't reply I just leave them unread to deal with at another point.

Lessons follow a structure too, starting with the folders.

> I have a really specific way that I give folders out and collect them in. Each row passes their folders to the end. They're in a pile there. From the back, they pass them forwards. They pile them up slanted. So it's just really easy to put them back at the end of each row.

Mel has gradually added more routines, more habits, to her day. In this, she is not unique. Plenty of teachers have routines for their folders or their uniform checks. Mel has built up her routines despite the fact 'that stuff doesn't come naturally to me.' Why does she do it then? 'It does make me feel like I'm more in control of the classroom.'

DOI: 10.4324/9781003453154-14

Problem

I don't want to start a free-will debate that I am not equipped for, but to what extent do you choose each of the actions that make up the hundreds of decisions whizzing past you each day? Or what proportion of those decisions are conscious decisions? We might be able to catch one or two, to hold them in our hands for a moment and ponder the merits of different options. Many will go unnoticed, not because we're uninterested but because the human mind can attend to only so much.

Our mental capacity, innate to all of us, makes powerful the pull of the default. If we always plan our lessons in a certain way, we're unlikely to deviate from that process. Even if that process is flawed or faulty. It's easy to know that planning explanation is important, that checking for understanding is vital, that clarity of instruction is crucial. It's harder to force those things in a space where routines already exist.

And so much of our day is made up of *routines that already exist.*

Where those routines are sharp, effective practices, where they've made us better or more efficient, that's great news. A baseline has been set that we're unlikely to drop below. Where those routines are the unthinking product of layers of action built on top of each other, there are likely to be better ways of doing things that are all but closed off to us.[1]

As one set of researchers describe, this is both bad news and good news. The good news? Automaticity 'frees up cognitive resources for additional processing and facilitates multitasking.' The bad? Habits can be prompted 'automatically by contextual cues in situations where they are unwanted or counterproductive.'[2] Because of this tension between positive and negative effects, David Feldon describes this as the 'double-edged sword' of automaticity.[3]

If you truly want to change, to improve some aspect of your teaching, you need to become an engineer of behaviour. Of your own behaviour. Far too often, and I speak from experience, we intend to change, to get better at something, but fail to do so because we haven't taken any of the necessary steps. Don't just watch the cogs of your day turn like it's a machine you have no control over. Don't stand back, thinking it's too complicated to change or *I can't fix this*. Start tinkering. Start small if you want. A cog here, a gear there. Seek out that small lever with the power to make big change.

That's what this chapter is about: engineering our behaviour. In the previous chapter, we saw how habits can be introduced through practice, repetition, iteration, and feedback. In this chapter, we'll consider how we can replace and overlay those already ingrained behaviours with habits which are more effective.

Solutions

Habitual behaviour doesn't have to be cold or unfeeling. From the moment Martha, teacher of Reception and Year 1, arrives in school to when the children come into her classroom, routine is central. Printing has happened the afternoon before so that the morning can be 'more about setting up the provision inside and outside', putting 'the books out ready for Maths,' and getting the 'date written on the board.'

Routines aren't just for Martha; the children know what is expected of them too. 'When they come in in the morning, they sign in by choosing a book... they want to hear me read later. They sit down. They write the date.' For some teachers, routines and habits accumulate gradually, a few good and a few bad. Others consider every moment intentionally and how it can contribute to the smooth, effective, and enjoyable running of the day. Perhaps because she works with the youngest children, Martha is in the latter camp. The children she works with appreciate the routine; they help and remind each other of it regularly.

Two routes to improved habits

It may sound simple, but there are two main solutions when we consider changing our behaviour:

- Introduce new habits
- Replace existing habits

Whilst this chapter will look at both, at least some research suggests that, rather than putting lots of mental effort into introducing
new behaviours, 'it is likely more promising to focus instead on replacing one habitual response with another.'[4]

Some of these behaviour-change strategies are described as nudges. Usually, these things are done *to us*. Governments and organisations nudge our behaviour: they try to make us live healthily, spend more, or pay tax on time. One pair of researchers reframed that, considering how we can nudge ourselves.[5] These researchers define these self-nudges as 'interventions that steer individuals' behaviours toward their ultimate goals'. Put simply, self-nudges are prompts and barriers we construct for ourselves to encourage our behaviour in one direction rather than another.

To change behaviour

The following principles draw on insights from behavioural science to help us to change. Some can be done with very little work on our part. Some require a bit more effort.

Make it easier

Surprisingly, where you put food in the fridge or the cupboard makes healthy eating more or less likely. More visible food is more likely to be consumed first.[6] Our biscuit tin is on the top shelf of a tall cupboard, and I still find myself reaching up there a little too often. It's not that this magically makes us healthy eaters, but defaults guide our behaviour. If we make something easier to do, we make it more likely to happen, and vice versa.

If we want to work in our classroom rather than the staffroom, leaving what we need to do our work in the classroom – planner, laptop, books, and so on – pulls us in that direction. If we want to start a new mini-whiteboard habit with one of our classes, having them ready on the end of rows is likely to prompt us more than their presence in the cupboard. If we want to model using the visualiser, having the programme running on our computer makes it more likely that we will use it.

Making it easier means planning. It means considering the barriers or the pitfalls and planning for them. Ask, 'What am I trying to change? What's getting in my way? What could I do in advance?'

Create a checklist

I once took a flight to the Scilly Isles off the southernmost tip of Cornwall. The plane was tiny, seating around 12 of us. Most fascinating was the ability to see both pilots from my seat in the middle of the plane. For several minutes before we even started to move, the pilots worked through a systematic process of checks. They flicked switches and checked gauges and various other things I didn't understand. Our pilots on the way out weren't excessively conscientious; an identical process happened on the return journey.

Surgeons and pilots, high-stakes jobs both, often work to checklists before operations and flights.[7] This surprised me at first: highly trained, well-educated professionals work through a list of things that they need to remember to do or to check. It jars with our sense of expertise. An expert should just *know*. It feels like they shouldn't need the checklist.

Where a problem is new or complex, where potential for error is high, a checklist makes expert action more likely. We aren't pilots or surgeons. Our job is complex, but the cost of error is much lower. A checklist can mitigate the risks of not changing, not embedding that new behaviour, or not getting to best practice.

How then might we make one? Ideally, *either* the items of the checklist will be fairly obvious to us *or* we'll be able to look beyond ourselves for these items, to a resource, book, or colleague.

If you know you want to change your start (or end) of the day routine, you probably have a clear idea of *how* you want to change. Your checklist for a morning routine might form itself into the following items:

- Organise books and resources for each lesson

- Check lesson resources

- Check to-do list

- Check email – Reply where possible/add to-do list if a longer response is needed

It's not that this is the *right* way to start the day. Many of us don't have the luxury of being in school early, so such a checklist might become the end-of-day routine. Either way, a checklist like this is the solution when the problem is disorganised lessons and lesson resources or an over-fixation with email. For a person who finds it difficult to reply to any emails, who feels like they're always mounting up, a 20-minute slot at the start of the day looking through them, making sure nothing's been missed, could be helpful.

It would be a mistake to see these as *just* about the way we work. Checklists can help us to shape and hone practices in the classroom as well. Quite understandably, many teachers often struggle to get and maintain the attention of the whole class consistently. A checklist for getting attention might look like this:

- Scan the room.
- Start a narrated countdown.
- Pause and narrate the positive between each number.
- Remind individuals by name where instructions aren't followed.
- Narrate the positive.
- Scan every seat in the room.

For some, the scripting and practice of the previous chapter could also help to do this. A checklist is a tool you *can* use. It isn't that every effective teacher is using a checklist to do everything (you know they aren't) but that checklists can be a useful way of embedding a new and complex behaviour or set of behaviours.

If children are constantly asking for help before they've really tried, we define practices that will encourage a little more independence.

Each independent task explanation includes

- A first step everyone understands
- Instructions on what to do if you get stuck/before asking for help
- Check for understanding of what students are doing
- Stay at the front of the room and scan for the first two minutes of any task/take no questions.
- Circulate – check that students have done the first step/done what they should have done before asking for help.

A checklist may, in its very nature, be a temporary tool. You use the checklist until you're happy that behaviour has changed. For example, that start-of-the-day routine checklist is temporary in that once you're in the routine, you don't need to refer to it again.

Be accountable

An action is more likely to happen, a behaviour more likely to change, if we know someone is going to check up on us. A friend, mentor, or line manager can help by holding us to a behaviour we commit to. They don't tell us what to do. Rather, they hold us to the change we're driving ourselves towards. Even better, if we try to change as a group, there's some evidence we're more likely to see that change happen.[8]

Equally, research suggests that the norms of a group are likely to influence your decisions.[9] If everyone in your team eats doughnuts at breaktime, it's difficult to opt out. This also works for positive behaviours: if you work in a team where teachers push themselves to know their subject well, you'll find it easier to push yourself in a similar way. Particularly important when choosing a school or a team, such research suggests that being part of a team you perceive to hold the behaviours you'd like to see more in yourself can aid you on the path to improvement.

Don't just seek accountability. Seek accountability from those you want to emulate. Find teachers you respect, whose classrooms inspire and challenge you. Watch them teach as much as possible. Or talk through their planning process or their organisation or the way they connect with parents. Tell one of these teachers what you're about to try with your class or ask them to check in with you at lunch or the end of the day about how it went.

What problem am I trying to solve?

As we draw to a close our time looking at behaviour change, consider our aim: *sustaining a successful career in teaching*. Any time we devote energy and effort to something, we're saying no to energy and effort we could spend elsewhere – an opportunity cost.

Time could be spent, energy expended, and all for a small change that hasn't helped us with our goal. Much of this depends on what problem we're trying to solve. If you want to maximise how you're using your time, get the most out of each day, and leave at a reasonable time, you find and embed behaviours that get you to the point where tasks are completed effectively and efficiently. A teacher who already is squeezing every second out of every day will see diminishing returns on efforts in this area. But devoting time to a change in classroom strategy might reap more rewards.

Key Takeaways

● Much of our day is made up of routines that already exist.

● It might be easier to replace subpar routines rather than try to add lots of new ones.

- Self-nudges are prompts and barriers we construct to change our behaviour.

- Self-nudges include making behaviour easier, using checklists, accountability, and tracking.

Notes

1 Habit experts Wendy Wood and David Neal point out that automatic effective behaviours deployed by experts are differently to our often unconscious habits but for practical purposes here we're going to treat them in similar ways, using nudges, practice, repetition, changes in the environment and accountability to change our behaviour. For further discussion see: Wood, W., and Neal, D. (2007). A new look at habits and the habit-goal interface. *American Psychological Association*, 114(4), 843–863.
2 Hobbiss, M., Sims, S., and Allen, R. (2021). Habit formation limits growth in teacher effectiveness: A review of converging evidence from neuroscience and social science. *Review of Education*, 9(1), 3–23.
3 Feldon, D. (2007). Cognitive load and classroom teaching: The double-edged sword of automaticity. *Educational Psychologist*, 42(3), 123–137.
4 Hobbiss, M., Sims, S., and Allen, R. Habit formation limits growth in teacher effectiveness: A review of converging evidence from neuroscience and social science.
5 Reijula, S., and Hertwig, R. (2022). Self-nudging and the citizen choice architect. *Behavioural Public Policy*, 6(1), 119–149.
6 Reijula, S., and Hertwig, R. Self-nudging and the citizen choice architect.
7 For a good summary of this, see Atul Gawande's *The Checklist Manifesto*.
8 Stead, L. F., Carroll, A. J., and Lancaster, T. (2017). Group behaviour therapy programmes for smoking cessation. *Cochrane Database of Systematic Reviews*, 3(3), CD001007. doi: 10.1002/14651858.CD001007.pub3.
9 Tankard, M., and Paluck, E. (2016). Norm perception as a vehicle for social change. *Social Issues and Policy Review*, 10(1), 181–211.

⚓ Embedding Habits – Notes for Leaders

Plan your work in light of human cognitive architecture. Leadership action and behaviour should be shaped by the truth that staff can't process large quantities of information in one go. In particular, when leaders want to promote certain behaviours or introduce new policies, an understanding of cognitive architecture can be a powerful and clarifying force.

How many times have you sat in a meeting or Inset (in-service training) where a leader goes through a complex new procedure, often for a relatively short period, expecting this to become reality immediately? How many times have you led a session like that?

The lessons of cognitive architecture and behaviour change suggest

- Breaking down new behaviours makes them easier for us to understand and embed.

- Models and checklists can help us understand the best version of a behaviour.

- Practice of behaviours makes automation more likely.

- Some practice can happen *outside of lessons* in isolation with specific and immediate feedback; other practice is happening, to a greater or lesser extent, all the time as we try things out in the classroom.

- Feedback that is specific and corrective can support behaviour change, as can praise for behaviours that are going right.

Imagine two schools are implementing a new behaviour policy.

In School A, the policy is explained on Inset, including some modelling by the Deputy Head. The policy with a guide for the language expected – Merit and Demerit – is emailed to staff. As term progresses, leaders go into lessons and find that the policy is not being used. The language was a change. Leaders knew that. But staff have been told what to do; why hasn't behaviour changed?

In School B, the process starts much the same. Except during the Inset the modelling is followed by explanations of what is expected. Staff are then – between

DOI: 10.4324/9781003453154-15

each model – expected to practise the phrases of the policy in pairs, quite casually. This is no big performance. Two leaders model some further examples of different behaviour scenarios and how to use the language. Term begins and staff spend time in their departments conducting further practice and checking each other's phrasing. A Deputy Head visits the meetings and addresses problems or concerns as well as modelling further and giving some feedback, confirmatory and corrective, to teachers. Leaders visit lessons frequently and give feedback, face to face, on whether the implementation in the classroom needs work or is working well. After half a term, the policy *is* going well, but leaders plan key moments to revisit it in meetings, training, and briefings in the following term.

It's obvious which school engineers the behaviour change, isn't it? But more schools I've experienced, including where I've been a leader, are like School A. In part, that is probably because we – school leaders – don't recognise what it really takes to change an organisation's behaviour. It's a comforting lie that *If I've said it, they'll do it.* Too often, this fuels an *us-and-them* attitude between leaders and teachers where staff are seen as lazy by the former and leaders are seen as out of touch by the latter.

If we want to make a big change, like changing a behaviour policy, there needs to be a big investment of time. Even a small change – if it's important to us – demands our attention on the active ingredients of behaviour change.

Nudge the routines you want. When the British government's Behavioural Insight's Team summarised the research on how organisations can 'nudge' behaviour of groups, they settled on four principles to follow:

- Make it easy.
- Make it attractive.
- Make it social.
- Make it timely.[1]

Leaders in schools could consider these principles when implementing a new approach or expected behaviour:

- We 'Make it easy' by reducing the hassle or by simplifying the message.
- We 'Make it attractive' by drawing attention to the right path, selling its benefits, and praising those that get it right.
- We 'Make it social' by showing that most people are on board or by harnessing the power of commitment to the team.
- We 'Make it timely' by prompting people when they are more likely or able to listen and by helping people plan.

A Head of Department, Lucy, wants her team to all use the newly designed booklets to teach the English curriculum. Not only that, she wants to use these booklets to improve some key aspects of how the English department teach.

To make it easy for the team, the Head of Department organises all the printing of these and delivers them to each teacher's room. Part of making it easy has been devoting meeting time in the lead-up to the launch to lots of questions and planning with the booklets. As the booklets are launched, Lucy aims to make it attractive by sending regular emails praising individuals and the team where it's going well. She aims to make this social by using this communication to emphasise how most are already making the change. Reminders can be timely if a leader circulates their team to encourage and support at the moment (or just before the moment) that the behaviour is going to be encouraged. A well-timed question – 'How are you finding using the visualiser?' – both offers support and gives a reminder when it can be acted on.

A phase leader, Tom, wants everyone to use mini-whiteboards to check student understanding of the sentence forms being taught. To make it easy, Tom goes round all four classrooms in his phase and checks that mini-whiteboard sets are available and ready to use. Fortunately, he does this before dictating anything to do with using the whiteboards as several classrooms don't have complete sets. Once everyone is ready to use them, he sells the benefits during a meeting. Tom has filmed himself and another leader using the boards to exemplify their usefulness. Several of the team have experience using them in some aspects of the curriculum but not more broadly. Tom asks about their experience and gives them time to share. Each member of the team commits to using whiteboards once a week for writing tasks. He uses these commitments to give low-key reminders of the commitment on the day teachers plan to use them. He makes the process social by using briefing time to update each other on progress.

Note

1 Behavioural Insights Team. (2014). EAST: Four simple ways to apply behaviour insights. https://www.bi.team/publications/east-four-simple-ways-to-apply-behavioural-insights/ (Accessed on 7/9/24).

PART 4
Reducing Workload

Problem	Solution
Chapter 9  We have to manage large quantities of work in a finite amount of time.	We must become experts in organising our time.
Chapter 10 The quantity expected of us is often unsustainable, unmanageable, and not conducive to effective teaching.	To focus on things that matter most and to improve wellbeing, we should reduce, not just manage, workload.

DOI: 10.4324/9781003453154-16

9 Management

Problem: We have to manage large quantities of work in a finite amount of time.	Solution We must become experts in organising our time.

Zoe appreciates the flexibility of her current school. She loves being able to get in early and leave when she wants. 'I'm marking before school. I very rarely take work home.' After this, Zoe makes 'sure supply is sorted' for her phase when it's needed. She uses the time before school to check 'any phone calls or messages that have come in overnight.' She also makes sure she's available to support her team and troubleshoot any issues before school.

At Zoe's school, PPA (planning, preparation, and assessment) is taken as a team. The main benefit of this? 'We share the workload'. Part of this is joint planning, but it's also about each individual responsibility. Each member of the team works for the others. For Zoe and the team, 'life is a lot is easier' when someone 'looks after English' and someone else 'looks after Maths.'

As Zoe works through the day, she adds things to her 'can do' list. Zoe tries to 'do most stuff on the day' so she can leave work at work. The list is one of the first things she looks at in the morning and decides what is important and what needs to get done; often she already knows.

Almost every teacher I spoke to had a different type of to-do list, a different routine, a different attitude to workload, but Zoe has set her day up to manage the workload likely to come in. Your job is to do the same: create a system that manages your workload in a way that works for you.

Problem

Recently, I was talking to a Head of Department who was worried about a member of his team. He said that this colleague was overworking because 'he doesn't know what to do.' It seems absurd to say a teacher 'doesn't know what to do'. There is

DOI: 10.4324/9781003453154-17

so much to do that we are never short of options. That, of course, is the problem. A wealth of options; a dearth of obvious starting points. There can be a tangible sense that you – as a teacher, whether new, experienced, or somewhere in between – don't know where to start or when to stop.

To begin with, we might think that *managing* workload is all we're trying to do, but management speaks of settling for where you are and just trying to deal with it. If you're fighting a three-headed monster, it might be nice if you had a good weapon to *manage* the fight. It would be nicer if the monster had fewer heads. Or if there wasn't a monster at all. So this section is split into two chapters: the first on *managing*, the second on *reducing*.

Managing is the solution when the problem is our struggle to be productive or effective. Reducing is the solution when the problem is that too much of our time is spent on tasks without value. Sometimes, these tasks have value but not in proportion to our efforts. Sometimes, they crowd out those things we want to get to but can't.

We know quite a lot about workload. Its presence at the forefront of teachers' minds means that this is an area rich in research.

We know

- Teachers are not satisfied with levels of workload.

- Teachers in England work a full day longer than their OECD (Organisation for Economic Co-operation and Development) counterparts.

- However, workload is not increasing. Levels of workload have remained stable.

- Teachers regularly work through lunch and other breaks.

- Around 40% of teachers usually work in the evening. One in ten usually works at the weekend.

I am not saying that teachers working through lunches or breaks, or choosing to work in the evening, are managing their work badly. Teachers should squeeze whatever flexibility we can out of teaching. Workload management is about increasing our satisfaction with the job. When we work for more than 55 hours in a week, performance suffers.[1] We're less likely to think clearly or make sound decisions. A long working week, one where you've gone above and beyond, can be a satisfying thing. We can look back tired but pleased at what we've achieved. Care should be taken, however, not to glory in or normalise the extended hours. Workload management is required to ensure that time spent is spent efficiently.

Solutions

Most secondary school teachers interested in career progression ultimately make the choice between a pastoral and a curriculum route. Whilst you aren't tied to a choice once you've made it, secondary teachers do tend to lean one way or the other from a relatively early point in their career.

Erin, a modern foreign languages (MFL) teacher was conscious she wanted to keep her options open. She was interested in MFL curriculum and had worked to develop the curriculum in her school, but she also liked the idea of pastoral support, taking on a year group and leaving her mark on them. She just didn't count on having to do both. Temporarily, Erin holds the position of Head of MFL and Head of Year 8, partly down to staffing and the need for Erin's expertise in both areas. Everyone agrees this is not a long-term solution, but that doesn't change the fact that, for now, Erin has massive quantities of work for both jobs that would intimidate most teachers.

Despite this, Erin's surprisingly calm about it. She talks me through a full day. It starts around 7 with emails and admin. By about 7:45, Erin is usually meeting with a parent, followed by a staff briefing, followed by duty on the gates, followed by visits to the tutor groups in her year. She might be teaching all day, including duties at break and lunch. Usually, she'll meet a parent after school and make some phone calls, leaving school around 6.

What has she done to make this manageable? Because of her Head of Year role, Erin's time before and after school are bookable by admin staff for meetings with parents. When she started, this meant Erin wasn't in control of her time in the way she would have liked. She would hope to have the end of the day to make calls only to find it filled with a meeting. 'I've blocked out 45 minutes on my calendar every day to make calls so that I don't have no time to do that until really late.' Now that time can't be taken. Erin has done the same during the day; if she knows she needs to work on the MFL curriculum or work with the MFL team, she'll 'block out time for department stuff.'

Finally, Erin has at least begun to master the art of saying no.

> This is something I did initially find difficult... So if people try to stop me in the corridor I'll say, "I'm really sorry I'm busy. Can you email me? Or can you catch me later? Or speak to someone else?" Because I can't realistically do it all.

Erin won't be doing both jobs forever, but, whilst she does, she can manage it because she's put in place systems and routines that prevent workload from spiralling out of control.

Solutions in this chapter are split into two. First, we examine a *principle* of managing workload; the idea is unpacked. Second, we examine the *practice* of applying that principle, looking at what real teachers do to mitigate and minimise and reduce their workload. You might want to skip the principle and move straight to the practice. This is understandable but potentially dangerous. The best managers of workload don't just do the right things; they have the right perspective.

Principle: Outsource remembering

Some of us live constantly on the cusp of remembering just one more thing we've forgotten to do. I used to realise I'd not done something days after I was supposed to have done it. Or days before a deadline I'd discover a mountain of work I hadn't known was necessary. Sometimes, colleagues would get up to go to a meeting and only in that moment would I realise that I was meant to go, too.

Workload feels intense because lots of it is whirling around us, slightly obscured by unhelpful practices. Deadlines aren't communicated. New initiatives and tasks are introduced in a morning briefing but with little specificity. It's unclear whether some jobs are *It would be nice if you could...* or *You have to do this...*

Quantity and clarity of workload may well be out of your control. When leaders are imprecise, unclear, or changeable, what can we do? Firstly, we can give feedback to this effect. Secondly, we can make up for what is lacking in communication or management of our workload by others by keeping a tight rein on the details ourselves. One way to do this is not to rely on your brain to retain everything which is chucked vaguely in your direction.

You can do this by doing three things:

- Stop trying to remember *everything*. Don't expect to remember tasks, messages, deadlines, or anything else *just because you want to.*

- Create a system that will record all the new information, requests, jobs, deadlines, and vague messages in one place.

- Use this system to manage your workload.

Practice: Outsource remembering

Having talked about to-do lists in Chapter 5, we're less concerned here about the medium or the form that system takes and more concerned about the principles by which we make the system effective.

The foundational principle underlying productivity guru David Allen's approach to *Getting Things Done* is to capture 'all the things that might need to get done or have usefulness for you – now, later, someday, big, little, or in-between – in a logical and trusted system outside your head and off your mind [his emphasis].'[2]

Allen offers a five-step process to organise all the information coming at us:

1. **Capture**. This is about gathering *everything*, 100% of the messages, tasks, and information that you need to remember. How we capture is up to us. Notebook, Word document, productivity app. These could all work. To truly capture, you must be certain you're retaining everything you need to. A collection of indeterminate Post-it notes isn't going to work nor is that crumpled piece of paper at the bottom of your bag.

2. **Clarify**. Allen offers a series of questions to help us discern what to do with what we've captured. Firstly, 'Is it actionable?' If so, 'What's the next action?' Allen encourages us to do any action that can be completed right away and in two minutes. If not, we can delegate or defer the action. Where the information doesn't fit into a neat next action, we might store it in another way: in a calendar, with notes about an ongoing project, or on a *remember* list.

3. **Organise**. Here, we order actions by what we can do *next*. Next communication with that parent, next bit of feedback for students, or next planning task. Some things might have to wait. *Read up on early brain development* might truly interesting to you but won't fit right now. It goes on. Allen also suggests that, as we organise, specific meetings or events and day-specific actions – things we have to do on a certain day – go onto the calendar. A promise to call a parent at the end of the week to update them on a situation can go onto the calendar, not for a particular time but just to complete on that day.

4. **Reflect**. Allen suggests regular review, including a more thorough weekly review. As we reflect and review, we can cut out things from our list that are no longer relevant, update our calendar, and also plan when these actions are going to be completed. This works well as a start- or end-of-week activity.

5. **Engage**. *Engage* is getting on with it. There's no *right* way to decide what to do on a Tuesday afternoon. As we look at further principles, we'll examine prioritising and focusing on highest-leverage actions. For now, it's worth remembering that we've organised incoming messages and tasks so that we can get on with them. The process should help us to have a near-perfect understanding of what we have to do.

Beyond the list

You can put everything on a list, you can capture it all, and still feel there's too much to do. The list doesn't reduce the quantity. Anytime we can do the thinking in advance to reduce the amount we need to hold in our heads, we're outsourcing remembering and helping out our future selves.

We can do this by

- Organising resources by year group, lesson, or topic (preferably ahead of time) and keeping them in the same place so we never have to worry about where they are and can check quickly we've got what's necessary. As far as is possible, own the space you have (even if you have to share it).

- Keeping track of any names we have to add to a behaviour system, positive or negative. Some teachers write these names on the board during the lesson but then have to rub them off to move on. A laminated seating plan can help to track these names without the need to get rid of them right away (a seating plan like this can also track questions). Other teachers I know take a picture of the names before getting rid of them. The important thing after this is to have some time to put on all the positive points and the consequences. Triaging these issues is vital: serious behaviour incidents need to be recorded quickly, and often a school's behaviour policy asks teachers to record behaviour incidents for that day by a certain time. Check through what needs to be dealt with immediately and what can be left to be added in bulk.

- Managing homework intake in a way that tracks who has done it, who hasn't, and what needs to happen next. Lots of schools have a *Homework Policy*, but this policy doesn't necessarily make it easy for staff to collect and track homework. Create a system – a spreadsheet which tracks completion, the back of your mark book (if you still use one). Lots of online systems do this for you. Use theirs. Don't just use it, though; know it inside out, understand what you'll input and why. Book time to return to it.

- We could set aside a notebook or a spreadsheet for notes on specific children for whom we know we'll have to contact home regularly. We capture everything about those children in one place. Once the information is captured, we devote a specific time each week to contact parents. The notes are ready, so we don't have to think or overthink through what we're going to say.

- Some individuals and some departments are notorious for their lack of file organisation. Folders have only cursory labels, and inside those folders, files with names like *Lesson 17 Version 2 USE THIS ONE* are the norm. *Outsourcing remembering* should apply to the organisation of our planning, and more often than not, this is now a process of file management. Help out your future self by labelling resources in a way that isn't infuriatingly opaque. You shouldn't have to find the right file through some Bletchley Park–level code-breaking.

Principle: Prioritise what's important

When you sit down to work during your PPA, how do you decide what to do? Or when you arrive in school in the morning, how do you start? It's not uncommon – it's really just a very human approach – to meander through whatever is on our mind. In fact, there's research to suggest that if we don't give it much thought, we're likely to end up starting with whatever's easiest. Even when, especially when, work is piling up, we tend towards whatever's easiest.[3] You can see why. The allure of crossing something off the list is powerful, particularly when that list is filling up.

The researchers go further, explaining

- As tasks increase, we prioritise the easier ones.

- When we select easier tasks, we complete work faster.

- But as workload increases, the benefit of completing easy tasks diminishes.

- By selecting easy tasks first, we often fill our time with them, diminishing overall productivity.

- We learn from, and get more done with, harder tasks.[4]

I can see this in my own work. I've kept some kind of to-do list for most of my career. I love sitting down at my desk and watching that list diminish. But, when I stand up again, sometimes the key problems I'm facing remain. The conversations I haven't had. The difficult class I've not worked out a breakthrough for. The planning conundrum left unsolved.

What can be done about what is effectively a bias towards easy tasks? In Chapter 5, we introduced the Eisenhower Matrix. A vital distinction the Matrix makes is between Urgent/Important tasks and Not Urgent/Important tasks. The latter is where we'll often see growth and development. If we leave them to chance, the latter will also likely be consigned to that solitary thought and wistful stare out of the window as the bell goes.

Others have framed this problem another way. We need to *eat the frog*, to do the task that is hardest or most important or most worrying for us *first*. If you get in early, do it first. If you don't get in early, do it in the first available time you have. Circumstance and timetabling may obstruct the *doing it first* mentality. You may need to teach Year 10 first. Where possible, though, we aim to *eat the frog*. Or as Carl Jung put it, though admittedly not about teacher productivity, 'where your fear is, there is your task.'

To some, the idea of having a priority feels a little detached from the experience of being a teacher. Large chunks of our day are not moveable. *My priority*, you might say, *is to turn up and teach well*. And it's true that this should be the priority of every teacher. Every leader should make enabling this their priority. To do that, you'll have to organise your day in such a way that reflects this or any other priority. Many of us claim to have priorities; few can look back on a day, seeing it as the purest evidence of keen focus on those priorities.

Priorities are easy when life is distraction-free. When a colleague wants a favour. When reception calls with *that* parent wanting another meeting. Even when we're enjoying something we know isn't a priority. These are the times priorities are tested. In every moment of our day – from the quiet calm before colleagues arrive through to the PPA on the noisiest corridor – there will be opportunities to push forward what is important or to lose your grip on it under the weight of distraction.

Practice: Prioritise what's important

Prioritise what's important is the kind of thing I used to write to myself at the top of my to-do list. Unsurprisingly, I'm not sure reminders like these really helped. The problem was that I *wanted* to do what was important but I hadn't *planned* to do what was important. What might that planning look like?

Parkinson's Law states that work will expand to fit the time and resources allotted for it. Where we dedicate a large portion of time to checking and responding to emails, to redesigning resources that are just about ready, to conducting lengthy marking or feedback activities, we're likely to find those tasks fill the time we give them.

If you've ever been amazed at how much you can get done in a PPA when you really *have to*, you've experienced Parkinson's Law. The same is true when you just had one lesson to plan on a Friday afternoon and found that one lesson took the whole period to plan. Meetings are particularly susceptible to Parkinson's Law. I've been disappointed so many times when a short agenda comes through for a meeting, hoping against all past experience that this meeting will have a length that reflects the agenda, only to watch each item expand into the usual allotted time.

To make sure we tackle those harder tasks, we have to act and plan intentionally. This means having a time, probably at the start or end of our week, when we look ahead and plan where all that work is going to fit. In that time, we can divide jobs into time slots we have. If you have an online to-do list, you can label and group the tasks, under the heading *Monday morning*, for example. If we want to really get to grips with a new mentoring system with a training teacher we're working with, give time to it where you'll have space to think and work everything out.

Schedule basic tasks. Time slots that are short, often wedged in the intervals between other activities – in the morning when we get in, the breaktime after our PPA – are great for getting little bits done. If there are some emails to respond to, some resources to organise, or some books to scan through, schedule this for those short moments between lessons.

Schedule important tasks. Basics are scheduled in appropriate slots to make sure we're free to do the harder bigger jobs. Space to think, particularly when we've got something difficult to do, cannot be underestimated.

The idea here is that blank space on our timetable is reduced, not so we're busily rushing from one task to the next. Rather, when we schedule tasks, we make our days and our weeks more intentionally planned, banishing the whims of each moment.

Different teachers will approach this differently. Head of English, Mel, always plans ahead, scheduling tasks for PPA. During these times, Mel's conscious she's going to 'start and not finish' jobs, so she chooses things where that's not a problem. Organising trips falls into that category, as does planning with resources she knows very well. If Mel's going to be planning something new or creating new resources, it'll happen in a period of uninterrupted, extended time, like after school or at the weekend. Mel's clear that she doesn't work every weekend or every evening, but she likes to schedule the tasks she enjoys for the weekend where she feels she needs to.

To many teachers, nothing seems wholly important, just as nothing seems wholly unimportant. Our work sits uncomfortably between the two. So the idea of 'scheduling important tasks' can feel faintly absurd. *What am I going to schedule? Planning?* But this is exactly how we should operate. Tasks which contribute more to student learning. Tasks which enhance rather than dampen our motivation. Tasks which solve future problems. Tasks which make it more likely we'll be better at our jobs next week. All of these things count as important.

It's true that these tasks don't form one, clear, homogenous group, distinct and separate from other work. What we do exists on a kind of spectrum from meaningless fluff to essential. Stop for a moment and play around with this spectrum. Make a list of five things you want to get done today or tomorrow. Rank them in order of importance. The top two can be scheduled.

Don't do everything. I worry here about writing a kind of *shirkers' charter*, but in the Eisenhower Matrix, there are two often-neglected boxes:

	Urgent	**Not Urgent**
Important	Do	Schedule
Not Important	Delegate	Don't

Teachers understandably might scoff at delegate. *Delegate to whom?* Equally, *Don't* feels wrong. *I have to do everything I've been asked to do.* Do you? And have we been *asked* to do all of these things? Or have we committed to them in our minds?

What do we do if we've scheduled our tasks, we've worked hard, and we've found that not everything has been completed? It's worth at this moment reflecting on the importance of the task. Did you not do it because it wasn't that important? If so, is it worth just ignoring? Did you not do it because you weren't sure where to start? If so, what is on your to-do list probably isn't the right thing. Perhaps there's someone to speak to or ask first.

In the next chapter, we'll examine more on what we don't do.

Principle: Focus

Whilst good teachers aim to keep classrooms distraction-free, school leaders understandably aren't asking themselves if staffrooms or workrooms are free from similar distractions. After all, teachers are adults; they should be able to direct their own work and manage their own time. I'm not sure I've worked in a school where teachers would welcome a silent staffroom policy.

But distraction is not a mild irritant. Distractions cost time and not just the time taken up by the distraction itself. When our work is interrupted by a distraction, it can take us up to 23 minutes to get back to the interrupted task.[5] And going back to your original task isn't as simple as switching your focus back on; as attention and work expert Gloria Mark puts it, 'there's a cognitive cost to an interruption.'

Avoid interruptions might feel like futile advice. Unfortunately, it's worse than that. Where are those interruptions coming from? I'd guess we'd place colleagues and students at the top of that list. The students running down the corridor we leave our room to challenge. Our class going out to forest school who clearly need help with their wellies. A colleague asks us if some printing left on the copier is ours.

Research of office workers found that they were interrupted by colleagues around three times an hour.[6] What's more shocking is that the same study found that we interrupt ourselves about nine times an hour. Another study found that we tend to switch task around every ten minutes.[7]

Intuitively, it makes sense that interrupted work will take longer to complete than uninterrupted work. But this isn't always the case. Some research suggests that during periods of significant interruption – from others or ourselves – we're likely to work faster to try to complete more tasks.[8]

We may well succeed, finishing what we planned to in a kind of frenzy, but at a cost. We pay for those interruptions with

- A sense that we're experiencing higher workload.

- An increased feeling of frustration, stress, and pressure.

- A feeling that you have to put in more effort to complete the same amount of work.[9]

Look at this list. Is that how your PPA time, before or after school time feels? If it does, then the problem we're tackling is our ability (or lack of ability) to focus, and, so far at least, all I've done is set up a problem. What can we actually do about it?

Practice: Focus

Cal Newport, computer science professor and working habits expert, offers a solution by contrasting two different modes of work:

- **Shallow work** includes 'non-cognitively demanding, logistical style tasks, often performed whilst distracted.'[10] Doing this kind of work doesn't look bad to colleagues; this is what lots of us are doing lots of the time. Newport argues that 'doing lots of stuff in a visible manner' – busyness – can become a proxy for productivity when we aren't sure what the indicators of productivity will be in a job where lots of our time will be spent thinking and planning.

For teachers, this is email, editing resources, sorting printing, and lots more. It's not that these are bad things or things we'll be able to give up wholesale. But we can spend whole days in this shallow mode.

● **Deep work**, by contrast, focuses on tasks that 'create new value' in an environment free from distraction. Such tasks are likely to 'improve your skill' and 'push your cognitive abilities to their limits.' Newport's main advice for setting up a deep-work habit is to 'move beyond good intentions and add routines and rituals to your working life designed to minimize the amount of your limited willpower necessary to transition into and maintain a state of unbroken concentration.'

For teachers, this will include developing knowledge of new and upcoming topics, examining student work, planning models, explanations, and questions. At times, this won't look like much. It might look like reading, sitting at a desk, or making notes.

Our focus on automation and habit should therefore help us to get to deep work rather than willing such work into existence. Consider what rules or routines you need to establish in order to enable deep work.

Things we've covered in this chapter so far that will enable deep work:

● Outsourcing remembering to reduce distraction.

● Define priorities to make clear where deep work is needed.

● Schedule times to complete necessary, shallow work.

● Schedule times to complete deep work. Going into a PPA where our aim is to focus on deeper tasks, we should be totally clear on what we're trying to focus on and what we hope to achieve.

Examples of rules we might establish to keep us focused on the deep and important tasks:

● Keep your phone in your bag or in a different room.

● When completing tasks that don't require a screen, don't sit in front of a screen. So, if you're reading a set of student books or annotating a resource for a lesson, turn off the screen, close your laptop, or move desk. (See the advice on email in Chapter 5.)

● Work where distraction is less likely. In a school, we're unlikely to find a place where distraction is entirely absent, but if we know that chat and gossip are features of a staff or workroom, these are probably best avoided for deeper work.

Key Takeaways

● Managing workload is just the foundation upon which we build a grander structure – workload reduction.

● *Outsource remembering* to reduce the stress of having to juggle lots of different tasks. You can also create systems that help you to track homework completion or other important data so that you aren't constantly reaching for those half-remembered jobs or issues.

● *Prioritise what's important* by consciously ordering your to-do list. Remember that, as humans, we're likely to preference what's easy but not necessarily important when we don't consciously choose. You can decide how to make these priorities, but student learning and your wellbeing are likely to feature.

● *Focus* by first recognising how much we switch tasks and distract ourselves (as well as being distracted by others). We can focus by scheduling the right tasks for the right slots. The idea of *deep work* – focused, challenging, and important tasks – might help us here. Distractions can be removed by considering the rules and routines we want to create for substantial tasks.

Notes

1 Virtanen, M., Singh-Manoux, A., Ferrie, J. E., Gimeno, D., Marmot, M. G., Elovainio, M., Jokela, M., Vahtera, J., and Kivimäki, M. (2009). Long working hours and cognitive function: The Whitehall II Study. *American Journal of Epidemiology*, 169(5), 596–605.
2 Allen, D. (2002). *Getting Things Done*. London: Piatkus Books.
3 KC, Diwas S., Staats, B. R., Kouchaki, M., and Gino, F. (2017). Task selection and workload: A focus on completing easy tasks hurts long-term performance. Harvard Business School Working Paper, No. 17–112.
4 KC, Diwas S., Staats, B. R., Kouchaki, M., and Gino, F. Task selection and workload: A focus on completing easy tasks hurts long-term performance.
5 Too many interruptions at work. (2006). *Gallup*. Accessed from https://news.gallup.com/businessjournal/23146/too-many-interruptions-work.aspx (accessed on 18/10/2023).
6 Wajcman, J., and Rose, E. (2011). Constant connectivity: Rethinking interruptions at work. *Organization Studies*, 32(7), 941–961.
7 Too many interruptions at work. *Gallup*.
8 Mark, G., Gudith, D., and Klocke, U. (2008). The cost of interrupted work: More speed and stress. In *Conference on Human Factors in Computing Systems – Proceedings*, pp. 107–110. doi: 10.1145/1357054.1357072.
9 Mark, G., Gudith, D., and Klocke, U. The cost of interrupted work: More speed and stress.
10 Newport, C. (2016). *Deep Work*. London: Piatakus.

10 Reduction

<table>
<tr>
<td></td>
<td>

Problem

The quantity expected of us is often unsustainable, unmanageable, and not conducive to effective teaching.

</td>
<td>

Solution

To focus on things that matter most and to improve wellbeing, we should reduce workload, not just manage it.

</td>
<td></td>
</tr>
</table>

Martha has a particular problem, unusual to most teachers, even many primary teachers. She teaches two year groups. And not just any year groups: Reception and Year 1. I ask a stupid question. *Won't that mean you're planning double? Doing twice the work?* She tells me that at times it is and has been. 'I used to spend hours planning. Hours. I'd be doing it on my weekends. I wouldn't have a life.'

Martha has wisdom to share on the very specific challenge of a two–year group class. But what Martha's learned from teaching these two year groups is applicable beyond this niche classroom set-up. When she has an extra busy day, when she knows this is going to happen, Martha doesn't stay late: 'I do what I need to do and then I go.' It wasn't always this way. 'I used to stay quite late every day. It would be okay for a few weeks and then I'd get quite tired and it would be too much.'

The job hasn't changed. The challenges remain. How has she managed this? Two things. First, 'Prioritising what's important.' Second, a change in attitude. Martha readily admits, 'I used to want to do everything myself.' Now, she's far more willing to use her teaching assistant but also the children. They are 'more independent than they used to be.'

Problem

To really consider how to *reduce* workload, not just manage it, we can't just dwell on the vast landscape of the problem; we need to map a route through it. To do this, we need to consider what kinds of workload are taking up our time unnecessarily, where workload can be cut back, and where leaders are responsible for untenable workload. And when we understand that – and I know that teachers already do – we need to attack the unnecessary with energy.

Often this problem is framed as a leadership problem: leaders asking too much of teachers or asking for wrong or inconsequential tasks to be completed too often. Undoubtedly, this is true in lots of schools, and, as we'll see, teachers do have to do a fair bit they consider inconsequential. That said, only 1 in 5 teachers feels that senior leaders are pressuring them to work long hours.[1] How do we interpret such a figure? Possibly in one of these ways:

- Teachers are their own worst enemies. They drive their own long hours.

- Leaders don't directly put pressure to work long hours but do create the conditions where long hours are likely.

It's possible that both are true and that these can be true across the profession to a greater and lesser extent in different schools.

Researcher Sam Sims offers some useful clarification when it comes to quantity of workload. He suggests, based on a large survey of teachers, that it isn't simply the quantity of work but the type of task that teachers are asked to complete. Sims describes how 'two-thirds of teachers reporting that they spend over half of their working time on tasks other than teaching' and having to complete tasks they see as unnecessary is a strong indicator of a teacher's 'intention to quit'.[2]

Unsurprisingly, this specific type of workload correlates with teacher stress levels. Teachers who agreed with statements like 'I am asked to do tasks which do not contribute to pupils' education' and 'data management gets in the way of teaching' reported far higher levels of stress than those who didn't think such statements reflected their experience.[3]

How much of what we do is unnecessary? It's hard to say, isn't it? Or perhaps, more accurately, it's hard to agree. A school leader might decide something is necessary; teachers might disagree. A mandate to call home every time a child gets in trouble might make a dent in behaviour problems a school is facing, but it's likely to cause masses of work for teachers with full timetables. Assessment and data tracking might lead to a richer understanding of students' learning and what to do about gaps in learning, but for the teacher marking endless assessments, quite quickly it will start to feel like a poor use of time.

What follows are some principles and practices to reduce workload as an individual teacher. To set out to implement any of these principles, we must believe and recognise that reducing workload is possible. We'll end our principles with a recognition that reducing workload isn't entirely in the hands of the individual teacher. So we'll examine how to become an expert in evaluating what is and isn't valuable to student learning and be able to feed this back to leaders.

Solutions

Clearcut workload categories aren't easy to come by. Whilst, at times, we might be able to say 'This task has meaning' and 'That one doesn't,' more often we deal with the shades in between. Leaders and schools may push us towards tasks we'd otherwise ignore. Colleagues can work in ways so far removed from us that they seem to be doing a different job. As such, the principles outlined here don't offer definitive answers to what must be done and what can be cut. Rather, they offer a framework within which to think about your workload.

Self-improvement books will often espouse the power of saying 'No'. To do less, we need to say 'No.' At times, this will be to an actual person. 'No, it isn't reasonable to expect me to have done *that* by *then.*' At times, we're saying no to the demands of the job or the demands we're making of ourselves. And that last point is crucial. You can begin to reduce workload only if you recognise you'll have to work in a way that could be contrary to what you currently feel is necessary, acceptable, or appropriate. The principles discussed here work only when we recognise they speak as much to our attitudes as they do to our actions.

Principle: Use the resources available

Schools and trusts approach curriculum design and delivery differently. So talking about shared planning can mean dramatically different things to different teachers. The teacher who *must* teach using the set PowerPoints and never deviate probably feels differently compared with the teacher who uses resources they've made in previous years or ones colleagues have shared to support each other. Imogen, teacher of Science, isn't forced to use a set of PowerPoints, but she ends up relying on what she's made before and the resources the Science department have pooled. Planning a day, four lessons at her school, can take as little as 30 minutes.

Some teachers will tell you that they can't plan using someone else's resources. Or that planning using someone else's resources takes just as long as starting from scratch. Or, understandably, that they enjoy planning and creating resources, so they don't want to leave it to someone else. This makes sense. Resources aren't the plan, so the substantive thinking involved in planning is left to do as we wade through the deep, often murky, waters of the hidden thoughts and plans of others.

Potential obvious routes to workload reduction, therefore, feel closed off to us, tempting but ultimately impassable. *It would be nice to use ready-made resources, but it's just too much work.* Erin, Head of MFL, points out that the shared resources in her department do save her a lot of time, but she recognises the privileged position she is in in having created lots of them herself for the department.

To ensure that the rest of the team are confident with the resources, Erin uses department time to plan together and unpack the content of the resources. This isn't so that everyone is teaching in the same way. Rather, it's to ensure everyone can feel the benefit of shared resources, the benefit both to workload and to thinking. Erin tells me, 'As head of department, I would never say I want to go into every room and see the same thing. We don't want scripts for the lessons.'

Debates about the quality of lessons planned using other teachers' resources rarely reach satisfying conclusions. We've all seen, and many of us have taught, lessons where the teacher appeared surprised by the direction the PowerPoint was taken. Each new slide brings about a slightly confused look as the teacher says, 'Right, we're doing this now, are we?' Equally unhelpful is the idea that the teacher can teach effective lessons only if they are taught using resources made from scratch.

For some teachers, it isn't that they can't plan with ready-made resources. It's that they don't want to. Planning is one of the more enjoyable and intellectually stimulating parts of the job. To hand that over to someone else feels like giving away something very precious. A totally understandable reaction but this enjoyment of planning doesn't have to be irreconcilable with using resources you haven't made yourself. As we look at the practice of *using the resources available*, we'll examine how this process still retains that intellectual work and creativity of thought that teachers love.

Practice: Use the resources available

Mel describes what kind of schemes of work she encountered when she started teaching. The instruction when she started wasn't 'Here's the scheme of work' or 'Here's the resources'; it was 'Here's the topic.' In this model, Mel describes how 'planning took ages.' There might have been some resources, but 'they were all over the place.' For Mel, 'The thing that's made the biggest difference is having well-resourced units.' This isn't about work being done by someone else. Mel recognises that she spends 'less time making resources' so that she can spend 'more time planning how I'm going to teach.'

Now that Mel is a Head of Department, she acknowledges that resources can be used badly. We dwell for a moment on the chaotic folders and shoddy PowerPoints we've encountered in the past. Mel isn't assuming that the presence of resources is going to make her team better teachers. The booklets acting as resources for Mel's curriculum come with notes for teachers.

Each booklet in Mel's department comes with teacher notes. This is the booklet effectively telling the teacher, 'You could do it this way or that way.' Mel has also made videos for her team about how to use the booklets and demonstrating how she uses them.

Booklets aren't the answer to your planning problems. Mel has found a way for them to work in her department. Other resources are available. A set of PowerPoints with example tasks as well as a guide for teachers can serve the same function. What's important is that it is clear to you how to use and adapt them. If there isn't a guide for teachers, go to the source, the person who made the resources. How would they use them? Does that fit with what you're trying to do?

If your attempts to adapt resources involves scrolling through a confusing maze of different versions of resources – PP Version 2, Lesson 3 PF, and so on – and it isn't clear which to use, the resources aren't helping. Or if your attempts to adapt resources involve staring at worksheets, PowerPoints, booklets, or curriculum overviews with an increasing sense that you've got no idea what to do with *this*, the resources aren't helping. If our only experience of using the resources available to us is this utterly frustrating dead end, we'd be forgiven for not seeing the point at delving back into them. But where we break through to the sweet spot of use and adaptation of resources we have access to, we save time and reduce what we need to do.

To effectively use lesson resources, we need to be able to answer the following questions:

Before we use/look at/start adapting the resources,

- What is the aim of the lesson? What content is essential?
- What should children know or be able to do by the end of the lesson?
- How does this lesson connect to previous and future learning?

As we plan with resources,

- How does this resource fit with the aims of my lesson?
- Are there any superfluous or unnecessary elements to the resource, including tasks and elements of design?
- Does this resource help me to teach in a way that works for me? Or does it force me into activities I feel less confident with?
- Does this resource reflect what I know about how learning happens?

We have been talking about *lesson resources* here, but we can probably stretch the definition of resources beyond that. Martha, teacher of the two–year group class, recognises the benefit of having at least some of the same children for a second year. She explains,

> When they come up to Year 1, we don't need to have that conversation with another teacher about where they are because I know where they are. I can be planning that in the summer for them ready for the new year. I feel more prepared.

Martha's knowledge of the children makes her life easier; she can work in advance of a new year in a way that she wouldn't be able to with a brand-new class.[4]

In this way, the children become the resource:

> The Year 1s help because they teach the new children in reception how [classroom routines work]. I'm not teaching everyone in the room how to come in in the morning, how to self-register. The Year 1s already know that. They actually enjoy helping the reception children.

What resources are available to you? Resources might be literal lesson materials. It might be the children you've taught before. It might be colleagues who can offer insight. How can what you have access to reduce what you have to do in the coming week?

Principle: Cut down and cut out

'What am I doing that I could stop doing?' doesn't seem like such a groundbreaking question. Most of us probably believe that if we *could* stop doing something – if there were a way to save time – we would have found it and done it by now. But when we're looking to improve or change something, humans are far more likely to consider *adding* a new practice or idea rather than *subtracting* an old one.[5] Within us, there exists a kind of blindness to cutting out what is already present.

It's easy to say *cut something out* and harder to do. To answer that question, we have to ask of everything we do, *What's essential?* Too often for teachers, *what's essential* is defined by someone else. And there are areas where control is beyond our grasp. But we can ask *What's essential?* of everything we do, from prep for parents' evenings to planning.

Greg McKeown, expert in doing 'less but better', challenges us to focus only on those things that are *essential*. He argues that 'You cannot overestimate the unimportance of practically everything.'[6] In this way, McKeown exhorts us to focus only on priorities. Eliminate those things which don't contribute or those things that don't contribute enough.

For teachers, this is a hard pill to swallow. Particularly, when 'practically everything' is dictated to us by our job description. If we look at our planning load or the jobs we have to do as a tutor, we might struggle to discern what's essential. Being a tutor *and* planning lessons are both essential. McKeown's message doesn't mean that you should stop doing all that you are doing. Instead, as teachers, we can look at the act of planning or the role of the tutor and ask ourselves *What's essential?* Of course, I still have to plan, but do I have to do it in the same way?

We can ask this question in general. When we feel overworked, when evenings and weekends are filling up, we can look at the specifics of our working life and ask 'What do I actually need to be doing?' If the answer is 'everything' (and I get that it might be), we must go to a line manager or team leader, a head teacher, or senior leader. We should explain the situation, and if they don't care or think that's just the lot of the teacher, they don't deserve us in our school. In my experience, teachers aren't reluctant workers; we're willing to work hard. At times, that might lead to quite unhealthy working practices becoming seen as normal.

We can also ask this question when we're about to start something new. A new school or role. A new project. A new focus for professional development. If I want to develop my feedback to students in the coming term, I might have to consider what I'm cutting back or cutting out to make room for it. If I've taken on a new responsibility, I might need to consider, at least for the time being, what the essentials are of being a tutor and stick only to them.

So we need to look at our work and ask 'What's essential?' Once we have an answer, we can start to *cut down and cut out*. Let's turn to look at what that might look like now.

Practice: Cut down and cut out

I used to over-prepare for parents' evenings. I'd had a couple of bad experiences where I didn't know enough and wanted to be ready with every answer to all possible questions. Notes would be scribbled on data sheets, notes I'd barely be able to read during the meetings. Asking 'What's essential?' could have helped me to strip back the extra prep I was doing. Class data was essential for me; everything else was a crutch I didn't need.

As in a lot of the areas I'll discuss cutting back, we're likely to be cutting back something that *could* have an impact. We do that for two reasons:

● We reduce the likelihood of burnout. Don't underestimate the power of freeing yourself from an incredibly draining commitment.

● We open up space for better work or other priorities. If every free moment is spent on the next set of books that need our attention, we're unlikely to get to grips with that difficult topic or try out that teaching strategy we heard about in training.

As Dylan Wiliam has said, 'In education, the only way to improve is to stop people doing good things, to give them time to do even better things.' Where do you need to give yourself the freedom to 'stop doing good things'?

Different types of cutting out (or stopping):

● Finding a shorter way to do an existing job

● Deciding not to do something anymore

● Reducing the frequency you do a regular task.

Areas ripe for cutting down or cutting out:

Marking and feedback. A school policy may limit your ability to cut this down. But such policies can often be bent rather than broken. I worked in a school where book marking was mandated fortnightly. Rather than provide excessive comments, I used codes to give students tasks that responded to what they weren't getting right. I did this because a more experienced teacher suggested it, and I found it saved me time. Hardly groundbreaking, it was amazing how the hegemony of The Policy means that lots of us just do what we think we have to rather than what we could do. Leaders at that school were perfectly happy with the code approach, but they hadn't communicated it, so lots of staff were still diligently writing fortnightly letters to everyone in their classes.

Advocates of marking will rightly point out that it does have an impact. Children can learn from written comments; they can respond to them, correct misconceptions, and enrich their understanding. Children may also appreciate written comments. They might notice the absence of such comments. I highlight this to point out the trade-off: we do lose something when we stop marking or mark less, but we gain something too. In almost no area is cutting back easy or straightforward.

There are two techniques that help us to cut back our marking:

1. **Whole-class feedback** can replace some or most of your marking load. It's not that we'll never mark. Certain pieces of work – that test or essay, perhaps – might warrant the attention that marking requires. Whole-class feedback is done very differently by different teachers and in different schools. Often, a whole-class feedback sheet will direct a teacher to make notes on specific areas as each book (or a sample) is examined. Common focus areas include mistakes and misconceptions, work to share with the class (and why), and specific students to support. Notes alone won't help the children, so whole-class feedback should involve some planning about what a class will do next time to improve, deepen understanding, or correct error. If you want to try whole-class feedback, do the following:

   ● **Choose a task** that you want to give some feedback on, something where the children are demonstrating knowledge and skill you've taught them.

   ● **Be clear on the success criteria** for the task by sharing it with the class, modelling it, and checking their understanding. For example, if the children are writing a paragraph, check that they understand the process by getting them to write their first sentence on mini-whiteboards and showing you. It's better to correct error before they do the task than after.

   ● **Choose a sample or look at the whole class**. Your decision here might depend on the task and the time you have. You might look at a range of abilities in your class. You might focus on the children who you know struggled the most with it. You might read everyone's work. We should be careful here to recognise the differences between different types of task. A paragraph demonstrating a specific skill can probably be sampled. A story each child in your class has put their heart and soul into shouldn't be.

- **Make notes** on the common errors, the successes, the children who need support, and good examples to share.

- **Plan a task** that helps the children improve. This could be an editing or revising task or a brand-new set of questions that will test the children's knowledge. Plan the explanation before the task to be clear and brief, explaining what the children are trying to improve. Perhaps plan to share a piece of successful work that the class can discuss before having their own go. Consider those you need to give extra support or challenge to during this task.

- **Evaluate the effectiveness** of whole-class feedback. You can't do it every time, but it's worth looking at the improvements you've made or checking understanding in a subsequent lesson. Have the children embedded the knowledge or skill you hoped they would?

2. **Live feedback** can only really be done in a classroom where behaviour is strong enough to allow you to focus on individual work as you move round the room. Live marking works best in those times when students are engaged in some kind of independent practice. We can try live marking by

- **Being clear on success criteria** (as above).

- **Giving the children time** to get started on the task. There's little you can help them with immediately unless there's an individual or group you support separately from the rest of the class. If you're able to scan the class before setting out into the room, you can check that expectations are being followed and behaviour is where you'd like it.

- **Tell them what you're looking for**. As you step out into the room, let the children know what you're looking for. Doug Lemov calls this 'Naming the Lap', helping you remind the class (and yourself) of the focus of that success criteria.

- **Choose the right tool for the job**. In lots of cases, this will be a pen but not always. A clipboard, mini-whiteboard or device to record errors can help you to plan a response for the whole class. You might tally the questions that students are getting wrong, so you know which to emphasise. You might take pictures of common errors as well as good examples to share with the class.

- **Respond** to individuals as well as the whole class. A balance between individual corrections and whole-class responses is hard to strike. You might start the same conversation with three children before realising there's a common mistake that could be more efficiently dealt with from the front. A response might be a modelled correction in a book, or it could be an explanation from the front of the room. It could be a conversation with an individual or a pair discussion of an error projected onto the screen.

Whole-class feedback and live marking work only if we cut down in other areas. Both can be impactful and time-saving strategies but only if we embrace them. If we cling to a marking load we should leave behind, neither strategy will help us.

Planning learning, not tasks. A restless mind is always looking for the *next thing*. A restless lesson planner is always looking for another task. Concerned with *filling the time*, we worry about whether there's enough to get through. Alternatively, the lure of an elaborate or different 'way in' to a topic prompts a tour of Facebook groups and Times Educational Supplement (TES) resources or a trawl of Dropbox folders and shared areas.

Simple teaching is neither drab nor lifeless. A simple approach to teaching simply looks for the most direct line between what is to be taught – the content or skill – and the manner in which it will be taught. The children need to understand a new concept? We explain it and ask lots of questions about it. The children need to embed a new skill? We isolate it and they practise it; we check that they've got it.

Resource creation and design. If planning your lesson sends you to the photocopier several times, that time could be saved. It's not that those resources aren't having *any* impact on learning. It's quite possible that they are. The problem is they're also having an impact on how much time you have.

When I was a newly qualified teacher, I made a sarcastic comment in a meeting about how long people spent designing their PowerPoints with pictures and animations. A colleague said, a little defensively, that her classes appreciated the work that went into those resources. Now, I'm not sure teachers are still spending an age tinkering with PowerPoint (if you are, stop), but the principle remains.

This is a principle backed by evidence. Cognitive load theory categorises the different kinds of thinking that we want (and don't want) students to do in our lessons. Intrinsic load refers to what we want students to focus on: the content or skill that we want them to develop. Extraneous load refers to anything additional or superfluous, anything likely to distract from the necessary focus that learning requires: conversations with friends, the teacher's joke over a silent class, or distracting details in the room or resources.

When it comes to resource creation, simplicity is faster and probably more effective. Some principles:

- Design should be simple. Superfluous icons, images, or text are unnecessary and possibly distracting.

- The resource should help children to understand or practise something they are learning (or revising).

- The resource shouldn't cause lots of unnecessary additional work for you. Spending hours at the guillotine is not a good use of your time. How can it be designed or printed to be ready to use right away? How can students get it ready to use?

Email. 'Send fewer emails' can feel like the kind of advice which is impractical and out of touch. (*I would if I could.*) But, if we want to receive fewer emails and have less to do with email altogether, we should aim to send fewer emails. What are some practical steps to making that happen?

- Don't reply to emails when (a) you're being asked a basic question and (b) you're going to see the person.

- Don't send emails when you have a basic question. Go and see the person.

- If you can't go and see the person but you can ask a question or reply to a question using an instant messaging software (e.g., Microsoft Teams), do that. Quick messages are better for quick questions.

- If you receive an email that is ambiguous as to whether an action is required from you, don't reply. If the information is useful – a deadline or *need to know* on a student – record it in a calendar or planner. Obvious exceptions exist. If the email is suggesting a safeguarding concern that hasn't been recorded properly, then you need to deal with it.

Contact with home. Good teachers have good relationships with home. You can't *not* have contact with home. School leaders also do right to commit to keep contact with parents swift and regular. How then can I talk about cutting it back? Contact with home is often a reactive act. A student misbehaves; a phone call is necessary. A parent has called in; you have to respond. In some weeks, you may have ten phone calls to make. In others, you may have none.

We can designate specific times for communication with home. Communication can feel relentless if we don't ever know when a call is coming in. Rather than always *react*, we can pre-emptively set aside time that is for contact with home – calls and emails – if we need it. It might be we have this time ready every Wednesday and Friday afternoon (so we can catch anything before we leave). That way, it's likely to never be more than two days before you respond to a parent. If you don't need the time, great – do something else. If you do, you're spending time more efficiently by doing everything in one go. One caveat: any safeguarding or bullying concern must jump up your list and can't be left.

Pointless practices

Unfortunately, there are some schools where teachers are sticking in lesson objectives into individual books until late into the night. Or are writing feedback in several different colours. Or filling your management information system (MIS) with data from a meaningless quiz every ten minutes. The main way these teachers could save time is, of course, known to them – Stop doing the pointless task – but this, of course, is harder to do than to say. Schools with high-threat, low-support culture aren't places where we want to challenge the pointless job we've been asked to do.

When we encounter such practices, we have a few options:

- **Do it**. We just get on with whatever we've been asked to do even if we find it mind-numbingly useless. Maybe it doesn't actually take loads of our time and so we decide to live with it. A word of caution, though: one meaningless task might be just about manageable; hours of them will destroy your motivation and your ability to get to the important work of being a teacher.

- **Feedback**. We try to explain the problems with a particular task or system. It's best to do this from a position of knowledge where possible, knowledge of the time we spent on the task, the problems we encountered, and so on. Knowledge of practice in other schools is also helpful. Other schools don't do fortnightly data entry; they have to do it only once a term. Other schools don't do laborious weekly marking; there's a whole-class feedback policy. Leaders may have responses to this feedback, and the issue might not go your way just because you've raised it once. Feedback does give you an opportunity to...

- **Ask how to fit it in**. If the conversation makes clear that leaders think this is an important practice you have to do, shift your focus to how it could happen. Genuinely look for ways to make it more possible but communicate the cost involved in focusing your time on X. *What should I stop doing or do less of to be able to do X?* Planning, marking, making phone calls home? A leader who can't see that a new initiative will take time when no new time has been created or one who thinks you should just fit in new jobs around all your existing jobs ad infinitum is a serious red flag on how a school is run.

- **Don't do it**. If we've exhausted the above options and, in particular, if *this* and everything else are dragging us towards a workload that is unsustainable, we can say 'Actually, I can't fit this in right now.' Each request should also be weighed in terms of what it is, who has asked for it, and when it has been asked for.

Not doing something might simply mean following the crowd who aren't doing it. It might mean taking a stand with a line manager. It might mean an attempt – you do mark books or phone parents but not to the degree the policy dictates.

Leaders shouldn't feel casual about asking teachers to do things they feel are pointless. Teachers aren't so common that a school leader should deal flippantly with one who is upset and being asked to do something they see as meaningless. If feedback, suggestion, or dialogue gets you nowhere, it may be time to look elsewhere.

The future of workload reduction

As more of a trend follower than a trend setter, I've never been the first to *get into anything*. To an extent, this approach serves the teacher looking to reduce workload well. Implementing fewer new ideas and learning fewer new systems win you time you would have spent working that stuff out. When we have enough evidence – from what we've read, witnessed, and understood – that an idea can work, we implement it with much less risk.

Given what I've already said, I was never likely to be an early adopter of Large Language Models (LLMs). The promise of artificial intelligence (AI), at times terrifying, confusing, and hopeful in equal measure, is one that feels a little removed from the day-to-day life of the teacher. Can an AI assistant reduce your workload? I tried to find out by spending an inordinate amount of time with ChatGPT and Bing. And that is the slight danger with using these platforms. What starts as workload reduction can quickly turn into playing as you try to figure out what it can and can't do. What it can and can't do is also likely to change and evolve. But this isn't some distant future. Teachers are already using AI. In 2023, nearly 1 in 5 have used it to help with school work in some way.[7]

Before I share the ideas, there's one more angle to consider. I was speaking to a friend about how I'd been playing around with these things and his reaction surprised me. I told him I'd written a draft letter to a parent (not one I was going to send). And he was a bit disappointed. Communication, he thought, loses something when manufactured by AI. I had been so caught up in the excitement of playing with a new toy that I hadn't thought about this angle. He's right, though: any use of AI needs to consider not just the ethics but what we value as individuals and teachers. Use of AI isn't value-neutral.

That said, an LLM can help you in a couple of areas:

Writing letters and emails. If you agonise over every word and worry about offending parents or failing to make your point, a first draft is waiting for you inside ChatGPT's elusive brain. I'm not suggesting you ping out letters and emails you don't read yourself. It's best to see AI as an assistant whose work we want to carefully review. I gave prompts on trip letters, whole staff emails on teaching and learning, letters writing up behaviour meetings and their actions. In each case, AI produced a letter that was close to workable if at times a little stiff.

In discussing *Outsourcing remembering* in the previous chapter, I pointed out that, if you know you're going to have to regular contact home about particular students, it's a good idea to proactively start collecting details about those students. If you store that electronically, you can copy it into ChatGPT and ask for an email to parents. Ponder a question for a moment. *How do you feel about that idea?* To some, it could appear underhanded to pass off the work of AI as your own. But remember, this is an assistant for you, not a replacement. You should read the email before you send it! You'll probably tweak it, cut a couple of sentences, and add another. But time you would have spent has been saved.

Writing worksheets and activities. AI struggled, at least initially, to write me usable worksheets. I asked for a worksheet where students would have to identify comma splicing, and it just spewed out ten comma-spliced sentences with a place for students to write their name at the top. My fault – the prompt hadn't been clear enough. I tried again, asking to mix in sentences where commas had been used correctly. Eventually, we got to a worksheet we were both happy with.

There is a problem with this example. I don't use a lot of worksheets in my teaching. In a way, I'm trying to force my teaching into a mould shaped by what I think AI can do. I do get students to do a fair bit of practice, so the worksheet model isn't totally wasted. In any subject where students might need to answer a lot of questions, AI can deliver.

At some point, LLMs might be more responsive and quicker to create high-quality resources. Even at that point, we might realise we don't need resources. They exist for us already.

Adapting resources. Many of us already have great resources to use. Planning from these resources can take time, but there's little help AI can give us with a task that's already been done. Instead, we might save time where resources need to be adapted to meet the needs of all of our learners. A page of text contains the knowledge you want students to understand, but you're teaching a class that struggles with reading this level of text. LLMs can take the text you already have and translate it into something readable.

Quizzes. QuestionWell is an AI model specifically designed to turn text into questions. If you have an article, booklet, or textbook page or story for children to read, if we want them to spend time thinking about that or we want to check that they've understood it, QuestionWell will generate questions for us. Although I might sound like a broken record, we will need to check these. They won't necessarily cover what the curriculum requires us to focus on, but, where such questions don't already exist, this could become a real time-saver.

Feedback. ChatGPT can already give your students feedback. Give it a paragraph, set of answers, or even an essay. Tell it what you're looking for and watch it digest a piece of work before diagnosing issues and suggesting next steps.

After looking at a *Macbeth* essay, ChatGPT suggested that I should 'Encourage the student to analyse the significance of specific quotations in more detail, explaining how they contribute to the theme.' This isn't wrong, but it's unlikely to be helpful. Again, the problem isn't really ChatGPT; it's my prompts. But you can't learn to write good prompts for feedback *in general*; often, these prompts will be specific to the task. As the LLMs learn, they will get better at this.

For Maths teachers, there already exists a range of programmes that can give feedback and diagnose potential problem areas. For the rest of us, AI might offer a way forward for feedback but probably only a tentative one.

Supporting individual students. I was speaking to a teacher recently who has a new student who speaks almost no English. She was despairing over the inadequacy of online translators and the difficulty of knowing where to start when it comes to translating a curriculum from one language into another. The student had access to a device and could converse with an LLM in their own language. Tentatively, the teacher is conducting a trial of lessons where the student can ask AI questions about content. The teacher will still be there to support the student, but AI adds another scaffold.

AI is, at least for now, a mixed blessing. If you learn to use it well and in the right circumstances, it may save you time, but his process can become a laborious journey down several blind alleys. As I started to use it, I became near-obsessed with tinkering, with refining my prompts and anticipating outcomes. Lots of this didn't reduce my workload. Looking at the clock and realising you've just lost 20 minutes in an effort to really refine a letter about an imaginary trip is not a good use of time. If this is likely to be you, I'd avoid it altogether. But if you're willing to try something, particularly if you have to write lots of emails or letters to parents, colleagues, or outside agencies, time can be saved. It's also that, even in the time it takes from writing this sentence to the publication of this book, AI will have improved its ability to do all of the above.

In the not-too-distant future, AI might be teaching our children at least some of the time, but the logistics of making that happen make it seem at least quite distant to me. Until then, if you want to, use it sparingly to tackle the jobs it can do well; if you enjoy the time you spend with it, perhaps spend more, refine your prompts, and get as much from it as you can.

AI will definitely evolve beyond what I've described above to the point where specific tools offer solutions to specific teacher problems. Such tools might be subject-specific assistants, markers, or resource creators. With at least some sense of the direction of travel for AI's applications to education, it is worth keeping an eye on developments as they emerge.

Key Takeaways

● We *reduce workload* for various reasons, both professional and personal. The pointless tasks we don't want to do, the ones that don't contribute to student learning.

- *Use the resources available to you* by learning to adapt the lesson planning – including booklets or PowerPoint – done by other teachers. Many will point out, quite rightly, that just opening up another teacher's resources and trying to teach with them is not planning. Some go further, suggesting that it is difficult (or perhaps impossible) to teach well using pre-made resources. But where resources can be explained – by a person or through notes and guides – and where they at least take us some of the way towards a fully resourced lesson, ready to teach, they can save us valuable time.

- *Cut down and cut out* is about deciding which activities have value to you and your students and which do not. A difficulty with cutting back is following through with it. We can intend to do less and still find ourselves looking at the clock, realising it's 6 p.m., having spent the last couple of hours making lots of phone calls to parents and crafting an email to a particularly difficult one.

- AI will undoubtedly change teacher workload, but AI-powered tools will change workload in different ways and at different rates. If it can help you now, use it.

Notes

1 TeacherTapp. (2020). Increasing the attainment gap, losing your autonomy and working long hours. Accessed from https://teachertapp.co.uk/articles/increasing-the-attainment-gap-losing-your-autonomy-and-working-long-hours/ (accessed on 17/11/2023).

2 Sims, S. (2023). Want happier teachers? Get rid of the fluff. *TES*. Accessed from https://www.tes.com/magazine/analysis/general/teacher-workload-wellbeing-cut-the-fluff (accessed on 8/9/2023).

3 Sims, S., and Jerrim, J. (2022). Understanding what makes some schools stressful places to work. *FFT Datalab*. Accessed from https://ffteducationdatalab.org.uk/2022/11/understanding-what-makes-some-schools-stressful-places-to-work/ (accessed on 17/11/2023).

4 There's evidence to suggest having a teacher teach the same class for a second year can benefit results, behaviour and attendance: Wedenoja, L., Papay, J., and Kraft, (2022). Second time's the charm? How sustained relationships from repeat student-teacher matches build academic and behavioral skills (EdWorkingPaper: 22–590).

5 Adams, G. S., Converse, B. A., Hales, A. H., and Klotz, L. E. (2021). People systematically overlook subtractive changes. *Nature*, 592, 258–261.

6 McKeown, G. (2014). *Essentialism: The Disciplined Pursuit of Less*. London: Virgin Books.

7 Education Intelligence Report. (2023). Oriel Square. Accessed from https://www.orielsquare.co.uk/wp-content/uploads/2023/10/Education-Intelligence_report_Summer-2023_digital-1.pdf (accessed on 17/11/2023).

⚙ Reducing Workload – Notes for Leaders

Imogen, a secondary science teacher, shares an instructive example for leaders looking to reduce staff workload. She talks about a phrase people use, and she's clear that it's 'not just senior leaders' who demonstrate lack of awareness of the day-to-day life of the teacher. She tells me, 'People say "This will just take a couple of minutes."' There's a pause before Imogen adds, 'And it never will.' Imogen's point isn't that no one should ever ask her to do anything or that all of leaders' requests should be doable in uniformly short chunks of time. She puts it like this: 'I don't think anyone has ever given me a task and said "This is going to take a lot of time and I'm really sorry."' As you think through the notes below, consider your framing of tasks with teachers and consider your awareness of the experience of their days.

Provide training on and time for adapting resources. When it comes to Continuing Professional Development (CPD), lots of schools have invested time in subject and phase teams. More time has been devoted to working closely with the people in the same block or on the same corridor as we are. Undoubtedly a good thing, this kind of time can be invaluable to teachers where it allows time to be devoted to essential tasks *and* supports individual development. In particular, shared planning allows teachers to interact with lesson resources in a way that makes them real and ready for the classroom.

Line managers should discuss how those times are used; they should visit the meetings and talk to teachers about what they're doing. Leaders should visit lessons and see the adaptations, discussion, and planning as they happen. The professional discourse in our school should be 'We have these resources – How are we using them to save time? How are we making sure they have an impact on our learners?'

Ask 'Is this for staff or for us?' When I talk to Steve, a Maths teacher nearing retirement, he mentions a positive change that he has noticed through his career, a change that is reducing workload. When Steve started, teaching and leadership felt 'all-controlling'. In Steve's words, in every area of teaching from planning to marking, 'People had to see what you were doing.' Now, Steve feels like the message from leaders is has changed: 'You're a professional teacher. I'll trust that you are a professional teacher. I will measure that professionalism in how you conduct yourselves... but I'm not going to micromanage what you're doing.'

In thinking about a leader's role in workload management and reduction, we need to consider how the leadership team's perception of workload is different from, and at times even at odds with, teaching staff views. How many leadership teams ask of every new initiative, data-gathering exercise, or curriculum planning overhaul 'Is this for staff or for us?' You might see a problem with the question; Shouldn't we ask 'Is this for students or for us?' Both are useful but the presence of such a question in our decision-making process is vital.

Tasks that take teachers away from the act of teaching are likely to be stress-inducing. Teachers are more likely to see data management, navigating complex systems for assessment and behaviour, or filling in arbitrarily complex feedback processes as unrelated to and unhelpful for the act of teaching.

Another way of framing this is through the question 'Can we explain why we want this?' If the answer offers purely monitoring, quality assurance, or administrative reasons, it isn't a good-enough answer, and the practice should be dropped or dramatically scaled back. If the answer includes some tangible benefit to student learning but staff just can't see it, conversations must happen to communicate the purpose and listen to objections. Teachers closer to the problem will have a truer sense of the practical implications of an initiative than most senior leaders.

Be reluctant to change. The risk of this advice is that reluctance to change when things are going badly – when lessons aren't good, when teachers aren't improving, when children aren't safe – could be catastrophic. But it's not simply about being willing to change when things are going badly and reluctant to change when things are going well. We must be wary of the change that brings with it a barrage of unintended follow-up tasks.

In 2019, in England, a new inspection framework was introduced by Ofsted (Office for Standards in Education, Children's Services and Skills). Curriculum was the focus. Neither the framework nor the focus was inherently bad. Schools should teach high-quality curricula. The introduction of the framework prompted a lot of work in schools. Some are quick to blame Ofsted for this; others blamed school leaders. *It wasn't the framework that was bad; it was the reaction to it*. It really doesn't matter. Curriculum work exploded. Some of this work was important, refining work of an area that had too long been neglected. Some of it was trying to distil your curriculum philosophy – whatever that means – into a document that very few would read. Some of it was creating garish, confounding curriculum roadmaps and timelines which made weak claims to clarify the curriculum journey that students were on. Some of it was meetings with leaders to discuss curriculum to prepare for possible meetings with Ofsted inspectors to discuss curriculum. Some of it was student voice, pulling students from their lessons – where we hope they'd be doing some learning – to talk to them about what they'd been learning.

Some of it was rebirthing curriculum resources which were fine as booklets or PowerPoints littered with a slew of unhelpful logos and text.

When a wave hits us – like a new Ofsted framework, a new CPD trend, or a new anything – we have only one opportunity to be reluctant. Waves like these are strong; if we let them, they will pull us along into an ever-increasing workload. When the waves are crashing down on you, ask

- Is this a priority for us? Do we need to do it this term or this academic year?

- Can we pause and see how it evolves or is implemented elsewhere?

- Can we spend the time discussing it, considering whether it's important for us or not?

Investigate AI. 'Investigate AI' doesn't mean spend a tonne of money on a shiny app no one will use. But some teachers in your school will be using AI; some will be aware of it but not sure how to use it. Leaders should have some awareness of AI, how it's developing, and how teachers in general are using it.

PART 5
Ensuring Success

DOI: 10.4324/9781003453154-20

Ensuring Success

Problem In teaching, there are many competing definitions of success.		**Solution** Define what success means for you (but don't hold the definition too tightly).

Steve experienced success outside of the classroom before he began teaching. He's coming to the end of his career in teaching. He now teaches half the week in what he describes as 'slowly finding myself a rhythm for the next stage of my life.' What will that look like? 'A blend of teaching and time with my wife.' But teaching isn't Steve's first career. Before he became a Maths teacher, Steve had a successful stint in business as a finance director.

Steve made the move for personal and professional reasons. He tells me, 'I knew I'd reached the limit of what I wanted to do in industry.' He had enjoyed what he'd done, been good at it, but didn't want to keep climbing. There was more than that, though.

> I wasn't actually doing anything. I wasn't making anything. I wasn't changing anything. All I was actually doing was monitoring and measuring what everybody else was doing. And I wanted to do something important in my life. Teaching was a way of me doing something.

Steve recognises the impact education has had on his life; he recognises how teachers helped him and thought it would be good to 'try and do that for other people from a similar background.'

In teaching, then, Steve has had a second successful career. The word 'successful' in that sentence could be taken in various ways. Steve has been a Head of Maths and Assistant Headteacher. He took these jobs because the opportunity was there and there was a need. They weren't what teaching was about for him, though.

DOI: 10.4324/9781003453154-21

I'm not looking to climb the ladder. I climbed the ladder because I thought I could do something useful for the school. The thing I have got excited about is working with students who really want to get on. Nothing I have ever done has been more pleasurable than that. Nothing.

Let's draw together the threads of both problems and solutions. In teaching, you aren't solving a single problem; a lone solution from one of the preceding chapters can help, but, on its own, it might leave the rest of your problems unsolved or even undefined.

Problem

What do you want from a teaching career? It sounds deep and slightly odd to ask the question. To some, progression is inevitable, the route we all should take. Promotion is at times seen this way because to receive recognition in the form of a higher salary, we must climb the career ladder. To others, teaching is about the classroom. Others still want to experience some of the success already mentioned but don't want teaching, the job, to take over their lives to the detriment of happiness elsewhere. Whichever route we take or thing we emphasise, we can, it feels, have little say over what we want or get out of a career in teaching.

Of vital importance, then, is understanding what success might look like in each of those domains, how we can achieve that success, and whether it's what we really want.

As we examine the problem of achieving and experiencing success as a teacher, we'll look at

- Classroom: what we're trying to achieve in our lessons and how

- Career: the difficulty with sustainable and successful progress

- Life: how we balance work and home

Classroom

The problem with success in the classroom is pinning it down. What does an effective teacher do? How do they engineer effective learning? Even as we begin to answer those questions, we realise that there is little agreement on what learning is or the kind of impact teachers should be having in the classroom.

In 2014, a report commissioned by the Sutton Trust, entitled *What makes great teaching?*, sought to summarise the research to answer that question. Their starting point? 'Great teaching is defined as that which leads to improved student progress.'[1]

That great teachers do more than simply engineer student progress hardly needs stating. Great teachers care, nurture, develop, and challenge their students. And lots more. Success as a teacher can be defined by the gradual accumulation of little victories with individuals.

Great classroom *teaching* is usefully defined, however, by the measurement of student progress. A dangerous misinterpretation of this would have the teacher obsessively measuring student progress at all-too-regular intervals. Instead, *What makes great teaching?* offers us best bets, the areas most worthy of our attention, if we want to accelerate student progress.

The report suggests two factors with the 'strongest evidence of improving attainment':

1. Content knowledge

2. Quality of instruction

If we're striving for success in the classroom, these offer two good bets as to how to reach it. Let's look at them in turn.

Content knowledge

The best teachers have 'deep knowledge of the subjects they teach,' and when 'teachers' knowledge falls below a certain level it is a significant impediment to students' learning.'[2] A wealth of research supports the idea that subject knowledge is important for effective teaching,[3] but this is not about accumulating academic knowledge, detached from the classroom. Teachers do need 'strong understanding of the material being taught,' but they also need to 'understand the ways students think about the content, be able to evaluate the thinking behind students' own methods, and identify students' common misconceptions.'[4]

What's the problem in all of this? The curse of knowledge is a bias grounded in the assumption that others know what you know. Experts can struggle to articulate their knowledge at a basic and understandable level because it is so embedded, so inherent to their ways of thinking, that they cannot help but work under the principle that others know at least some of what they know.[5]

If you've been teaching for any length of time, you've probably catalogued, maybe implicitly, a host of ways that students get lost in your subject. Understanding how children misunderstand within the domain we're teaching is essential. It's not too complicated to understand, in theory, how students get stuck. What's harder, and more illusory, is developing knowledge of what the students in front of you know in any given moment and how that knowledge aligns with or diverges from what the curriculum demands of them.

When Wiliam and Black wrote their seminal work on formative assessment, they used the metaphor of the black box because teachers input, through explanation, activities, and so on, and the box produces outputs, like knowledge, results, or feelings of achievement, but we don't necessarily know what is happening in the box.[6] Content knowledge won't mean very much unless we can use it to hold a mirror to what students are understanding.

Quality of instruction

One route many teachers are taking to achieve classroom success is to base decisions in the classroom on research. The authors of *What makes great teaching?* suggest three sources of evidence if we want to base our understanding about teacher effectiveness on the research available:

- Evidence about effective teacher behaviours

- Evidence from studies that demonstrate the effectiveness of an intervention that teachers can use

- Evidence from cognitive science that can be applied directly to the classroom.[7]

Is classroom success, therefore, simply applying the evidence as we find it? Several problems make this tricky. Research is not always readily available or easily accessible. A principle from research might slot easily into one subject or phase but not another.

What makes great teaching? suggests that the classroom strategies that will have the most impact include

- Asking a high number of questions to *all* students in the class

- Reviewing previous learning

- Modelling responses to the class

- Retrieval and spaced practice.

Less effective practices include

- Being overly lavish with praise

- Allowing learners to 'discover ideas themselves'

- Teaching to a 'preferred learning style.'

Great teaching, however we understand it, probably can't be captured perfectly in a few bullet points. The power of research is the direction it points us in the classroom. But knowledge alone isn't sufficient. We can know that our questions should reach every student in the class, but we may struggle to make that happen with a tricky class. We can know we should review prior learning but not be sure what to review or how. We can do things supported by 'the research' but become discouraged when they don't bring about the dramatic change, the dramatic success, we were hoping for.

Our problem, then, is translating best practice into our practice, moving evidence from theory to reality, no easy task in the swirl of new initiatives and easy fixes that float in and out of our schools.

Career

Success in the classroom should precede successful career progression. Credibility is won by leaders who have a clear sense of what it means to be a busy teacher. A tutor on a busy teaching day can't solve every behaviour issue in their tutor group. A teacher new to a key stage can't do everyone's Maths planning right away. Although it's a truism, it's probably best to do the job well before seeking to lead others. A problem with that is, as with many professions, doing the job well doesn't exactly prepare you for leading others.

The Peter Principle is the observation that we tend to rise, in terms of promotion, to the level of our incompetence. Workers are promoted based, largely, on previous success, but previous success in one job isn't necessarily the best determiner of success in another. At least in some industries, this isn't just a theory but a reality. In sales, for example, the best sales people don't necessarily make the best managers.[8] Coupled with the Dunning–Kruger effect, our tendency to overestimate our abilities, the Peter Principle is a stark warning of rushing to the next role and then the next. We often don't know our abilities as well as we think we do.

Dunning–Kruger in reverse is Imposter Syndrome or Imposter Phenomenon, where we doubt our abilities or fear being uncovered as a fraud. One survey found that well over half of professionals experienced Imposter Syndrome in some way.[9] Whilst the warning of the Peter Principle is not to rush to promotion, Imposter Syndrome is likely to make us reluctant to move forward or, when we achieve a promotion, cause us to feel uncomfortable in the new role.

At times, career progression for me has felt like those computer games I played as a child. You're jumping from one platform to the next, hoping the ground doesn't crumble beneath your feet before you're ready to move forward.

Life

One further problem of career progression is the fresh imbalance it can bring to our lives. We had a routine; the new job crushes it. Imogen, secondary science teacher, sees this clearly in our conversation. 'It's awful but I think you have to be really, really devoted to be going into senior leadership... The money you get is not worth the time you're putting in.' For this reason, Imogen is 'hesitant to progress much further.' She recognises that at a certain point in that progression, she'd be sacrificing 'emotional and social wellbeing for a job.'

Mari, Head of History, had a similar experience when she came back from maternity leave.

When I was pregnant with my daughter, I was going to come back as head of department full time. I had her and I knew that because I am who I am that I was never going to be able to do both... I relinquished responsibility and focused on my daughter.

I'm not really going to talk to you about *Ensuring Success* in life in general, because you're an adult and that can be defined and pursued by you. But, as someone who has sought promotion fairly regularly, I see the wisdom in those teachers who haven't done so on purpose, because they know the decision is right for their wellbeing.

Not seeking promotion is one way of finding balance between work and life. Another is being selective in where you work. Zoe, Year 6 teacher, recognised early that some schools were less flexible than others. 'In a lot of schools, you've got to be in by a certain time and that doesn't always work with a family.' Equally, in those schools, 'If you've left before 4.30, something's wrong.' These attitudes are likely to dissuade colleagues with young families from feeling settled and happy and ultimately staying in a school. For Zoe, when looking for a school, 'Having that trust [from leaders] is so important.'

Ultimately, our views of teaching are likely to shape how it interacts with our lives. Mari offers the advice she gives to less experienced colleagues: 'I've always said to everyone that if you were to leave you'd be replaced in a heartbeat. The most important relationships you'll have are with your own family and friends.' But, in our conversation, Mari recognises that she doesn't always follow this advice herself; teaching is all-consuming for her, largely because 'It's a vocation rather than a profession. It's something that I believe you have to have a passion for.' A sense of vocation is probably what prompts Mari to work evenings and weekends pretty regularly.

Imogen sees teaching slightly differently. There is a hint of vocation when she tells me, 'I'm not in this job for the money otherwise I'd be elsewhere. I genuinely do love it.' But she's taken steps to ensure there is a clear dividing line between work and life. Imogen works quite a long day but then doesn't work at home: 'I really try not to do any work at home. The reason I'm starting early and leaving late is so that when I go home that is home and I'm done.' Imogen has made decisions about how she wants to think about work (or not) when she isn't at work. 'I turn my emails off after five o clock. If I'm still at school I'll see them. If I'm at home I won't. I don't look at work emails over the weekend.'

It's not that one of these teachers is doing the right thing and one has got it wrong. Some teachers I interviewed genuinely seemed to want to work in the evenings and at weekends. We should stop and question whether we *have* to work in the way that we are if this is case. Equally, if we're out the door early, we could reflect on whether there's more we could be doing to find success at work. Questioning and reflecting help us to step out of ourselves and consider if the current reality we're living with is actually what we want.

One teacher I interviewed recognised that her perfectionism was really sapping the energy from the rest of her life. I asked her if there was a switch she could flick to turn off that perfectionism, would she do it? A moment's hesitation followed. The perfectionism, the hard work, was so tied to what being a teacher is to this person that the idea of the switch didn't quite make sense. Of course, she wanted more time to relax, more time with friends and family, but she wanted to be a teacher as she is. Easy answers for this teacher, and the many like her, don't exist. If we want a change in the way work balances with life, we can work for it, but we may have to accept a different kind of work for a different kind of life.

Solutions

For some teachers, the progress made is more tangible than for others. Martha teaches children in reception, and the early wins with these children are some of the most rewarding.

> When they start, they can't hold a pencil... Even by Christmas, they're writing. And then by the summer, they're writing short stories. It's amazing. Sometimes I have to remind myself and look back. That's where they were and this is where they are.

Although this success is unique to Martha's classroom, all teachers can point to some kind of success in the progress being made with class or classes.

As we examine success as a teacher, it's worth keeping hold of those three domains we've already mentioned:

- Classroom

- Career

- Life

Some solutions might work better or appeal more than others. Let's look at them again in turn and consider how we can reach the success we're after.

Classroom

Whole books, training schemes, and keynote speeches have been written and delivered about this kind of success. We don't have that kind of time, but we can take solace in the fact that teaching is both very simple and incredibly complex. It's simple in that we can understand what we have to do to be successful almost immediately. That said, it takes a career to refine and reach for this success. Often, success remains elusive or feels frustratingly momentary.

Here are some best bets for success in the classroom:

- **Develop knowledge**. Knowledge is privileged in that the better we understand the curriculum and the students we are teaching, the more effective a teacher we seem to become.[10] Developing knowledge doesn't have to mean we sit in a dusty room reading dustier tomes. Academic has, at times, become a synonym for detached, irrelevant, or practical knowledge. Teacher knowledge must be tied to its uses in the classroom. Understand what students should know, deeply understand it so you can explain it, and then understand how they might struggle to grasp that. Acquiring this knowledge might, at times, look like reading books, blogs, articles, and resources. At others, it might come from reading through the work students have produced. At others still, such knowledge can be acquired only in the classroom as we take answers, discuss, and circulate.

- **Understand the evidence**. When I first became aware that a field like cognitive science might have something quite significant to say to the individual teacher (as well as school leaders), I was, to put it mildly, a little frustrated no one had brought it up before. If I'd just known this sooner, I would have been a better teacher. I'm not really sure this would have been the case, but a grounding in evidence offers best bets and things to avoid in the classroom. 'The evidence' isn't something you can read, understand, and then simply apply. Each classroom, subject, and child is different. Being an evidence-informed teacher is not the same as being an absolutist, refusing to budge or change from what you've read.

- **Be an expert in behaviour change**. In Part 2, we looked at how we change our behaviour. What I hope was clear is that it's remarkably hard to do. Success in the classroom is inextricably linked to our ability to learn, adapt, and change to the present challenges and to new ones. Return to takeaways in Part 2 and consider what you can apply to take the next step to improve your classroom practice.

One way to engineer feelings of success in the classroom (and beyond) is to focus in on them to make sure, in the rush of work and life, we don't miss them. Head of English Mel admits she was hard on herself to start with. She explains what she did to combat this negativity:

> I started to write down three good things every day. It might be like 'I had a good lesson with a tricky student or Someone in my tutor group was upset and I was able to help them.' In everyday, there will always be three things that have been a success. I did it for ages every day without fail. That was brilliant because I got to a point where I'm able to notice that there have been positives.

Mel doesn't still do this, because, as she says, practising it for a while helped her to develop a perspective which is better at noticing the positive in each day.

Career

Harness the Peter Principle

If we know that people are often promoted beyond their abilities, every promotion we consider could be seen differently. As well as seeing the opportunity, the responsibility, the power, and the small amount of extra cash, we might see the potential dangers, the deficits in our experience, or the challenges we have yet to confront. My point is not that these things should put us off entirely but that they should give us pause for thought.

Erin, Head of Modern Foreign Language (MFL) and Head of Year 8, gives this helpful advice when discussing career progression: 'Speak to people who do that job. Shadow someone.' This is how Erin decided that pastoral leadership could work for her. She also asked trusted colleagues if they could see her in the pastoral role. As Erin says, 'Without seeing it, you don't know what the job's like.' We can think we've seen it because we work with a phase leader or head of year, but if we haven't spent time with these people, if we haven't asked them what their days look like, we might have a mistaken idea of what the role involves.

The Peter Principle is less likely to be our reality if we're ready for a job, we know it well, and, out of that knowledge, we're preparing for the specific challenges it poses. If you want to progress to a specific job:

- Meet with someone who does it.

- Ask them what their day involves.

- Ask them the biggest challenges in their job.

- Ask them what they wish they'd known when they started.

- Compare what they tell you with your knowledge of yourself.

- Reflect on whether you'd enjoy the job and whether you feel ready for the challenges they describe.

- Speak to a trusted colleague or friend about how you match up with their description of the job.

Coach Brad Stulburg offers useful advice to those wanting to progress. 'Progress in anything, large or small, requires recognising, accepting and starting where you are. Not where you want to be. Not where you think you should be.' [11] For Stulburg, acceptance is a necessary prerequisite of growth; it is 'taking stock of a situation and seeing it clearly for what it is – whether you like it or not.' It's only then that we can figure out and 'take wise and productive action to get to where you want to go.'

Harness imposter syndrome

Imposter Syndrome stems from a high expectation of ourselves that we're uncertain of meeting. Every perceived failure or setback, every missing of the mark, can feel like an assault on those expectations and the understanding we have of ourselves.

Imposter Syndrome drags our attention towards what others may be thinking of us. We relive moments of embarrassment or failure and believe that the witnesses of these moments think about them as much as we do. However, there's strong evidence that we dramatically overestimate how observers evaluate us both when we succeed and when we fail. We tend to assume others are rating our performance based on one-off events, but observers don't tend to make generalised judgements based on individual wins or losses.[12]

Psychologist Ethan Kross suggests that these negative thoughts about failures or mistakes and what others might think of them do more than simply make us miserable. He describes 'chatter' as 'cyclical negative thoughts and emotions that turn our singular capacity for introspection into a curse rather than a blessing.'[13] Such thoughts diminish our capability to focus or work productively as they monopolise the attention of our working memory.

Kross suggests that putting distance between you and such thoughts is a crucial way to tackle chatter and Imposter Syndrome. This distance can be

- **Fly on the wall**: Kross conducted an experiment where individuals had been asked to relive or think through a difficult memory. In this experiment, one group relived the memory simply as they remember it, from their own perspective and in the first person. Another group were asked to view the memory from an outsider or observer perspective. This second group were better able to detach from the potential upset or embarrassment of the memory and consider the big picture. They also began to learn from the alternate perspective. . Distancing in this way shortened the periods in which participants experienced negative emotions.[14]

- **Chronological**: Temporal distancing involves 'time travelling into the future' and considering how you'll feel about a situation, failure, or mistake in ten years' time. Kross explains that 'Doing so leads people to understand that their experiences are temporary, which provides them with hope.'

We often say to ourselves or others 'I need to get some perspective' or 'Put it in perspective.' Given the evidence from psychology, this could be good advice, but, as it turns out, the best perspective to overcome the negative thoughts dragging us down is probably one of detachment.

If you frequently experience these thoughts, it's probably best to talk it through with someone you trust and explain how you're feeling. You can also start to practise the detached perspective by forcing yourself to think through a situation as an observer or travel into the future and consider how you'll feel about an event in ten years' time.

Life

Be clear on what success means for you

During my interviews, I spoke to several teachers who were closing in on retirement. Several of these teachers had held positions of responsibility in school, including senior responsibility. None of them, when asked, viewed the success they'd achieved as a teacher through the lens of career advancement. None of them looked back wistfully on the Senior Leadership Team (SLT) meeting or the challenging professional conversations. None of them thought, 'I knew I'd really made it as a teacher when the policy I'd written was approved by governors.' It isn't that these things are unimportant. They are vital but it seems unlikely that we will be measuring our success as a teacher against the paraphernalia surrounding the responsibilities we accrue. Success for these teachers, and those with less experience, was closely tied to triumphs with individual students and classes. Breakthroughs in behaviour and understanding ranked more highly when I asked teachers what success in their job looked like to them.

If we're clear on what success looks like for us, at least in the present, we can adapt our teaching approach accordingly. It's not that this approach can't change. If you define what that success looks like for you now, you can remind yourself when you feel a pull towards a different version of success you're either imposing on yourself or having imposed on you.

Success could be 'Working towards a subject leader position' across your school. Or it could be 'Being able to come home earlier on Thursday and Friday' to spend time with family. Or perhaps it's 'Understanding and teaching the new curriculum as well as I can.' If your idea of success doesn't include a promotion in the near future, you don't have to work for that; you don't have to feel the quiet desperation to reach that role as soon as possible or to feel the niggle when a friend is promoted and is feeling excited about it.

Focus on what you're giving more than what you're getting

Is teaching a vocation or a profession? It probably depends on who you ask. The difference is sometimes conceived of as innate skill and passion versus experience and expertise. At times, teaching feels as though it's pulling towards profession with the higher and higher expectation of knowledge and expertise as well as relatively high-stakes accountability frameworks. Of course, at others, it's clearly a vocation in that it demands so much of us: our energy, our time, our emotions.

One teacher I interviewed told me, 'It's a vocation rather than a profession. It's something that I believe you have to have a passion for otherwise you'll come in but then leave quite quickly.' I'm not sure I agree. It's true that passion and excitement for young people, for learning, and for our subjects are valuable drivers of both our own motivation and success in the classroom. It is good for teachers to be passionate. But I can't believe in a view of teaching which demands we sacrifice our lives in order to be successful.

There may be days or terms or years when teaching for you is a vocation. It is, in those times, about going above and beyond for our class or classes. It is a really hard slog working for the best for the children in front of you. And then, through the varied circumstances of life, there might be times when it comes to be more of a profession, one where we do work hard but are able to switch off.

There is one facet of vocation that might be helpful as we conclude our discussion of success. We're told, 'It's better to give than to receive.' As well as a philosophical or spiritual statement, it seems this is also research-based. When we get or experience new things, we do experience genuine happiness. An increase in income, a new gadget, a promotion, all of these bring us happiness. But the happiness experienced is, if not momentary, then at least temporary.[15] The job or role we were striving for can feel like everything until we're in it and we realise some of the same challenges exist as do some new ones. We thought perhaps we'd *made it* when the promotion came around, but, a few months in, we're wondering what's next. The happiness we experience from receiving or gaining something is likely to diminish.

In contrast, the feeling of happiness that comes from giving to others, including helping others, takes longer to disappear.[16] Teaching, at its heart, is helping others. Helping them to do something new, understand something new, to take a few more steps towards maturity. Perhaps that's why so many teachers enjoy the classroom. It brings a kind of happiness that lasts a little longer.

Steve, who'd arrived in teaching from business, puts it like this. 'My other jobs had highs and lows.' Steve points out, because we often experience them alone, because it's so tied to the often-frustrated progress of young people, that 'the lows in teaching are lower' than his job in business. But he's clear that he wouldn't exchange those extremes, because 'the highs are higher' in teaching, often so much higher.

Key Takeaways

- Every teacher has a different understanding of success. These understandings change, develop, and respond to circumstances. Similarly, teaching is a vocation for many but not for all. For some, it is a vocation during some periods but not in others. A teacher may start full of enthusiasm and energy, going above and beyond with their class and loving it, but personal circumstances might mean that, for a time at least, remaining as this kind of teacher is not possible.

- Success in teaching could be classified into three areas: classroom, career, and life. Depending on the teacher, each of these will be more or less important.

● Most teachers set out to achieve success in the classroom. For some, not all, this gives way to seeking success in terms of career progression. We should remember that, for many teachers, such progression doesn't look or feel like success at all. These teachers don't want to move away from the thing they joined the profession for: the classroom, the craft, and the children.

● Career progression should rarely be rushed. The dangers of Dunning–Kruger, an overestimation of our abilities, and the Peter Principle, and the tendency to be promoted beyond our level of competence warn against progression without development or success in our current position.

● Experienced teachers tend not to look back fondly at the mechanics or administration of teaching and leadership roles. Most teachers' understanding of success, and the thing that research suggests will give us the most satisfaction, is the difference that we make.

● Most teachers want a career that works with their life, that allows them time for friends, family, and interests, and that doesn't drain every ounce of energy by the end of each day. The research and our experience are clear: teachers are willing to work and work very hard.

Notes

1 Coe, R., Aloisi, C, Higgins, S., and Elliot Major, L. (2014). *What Makes Great Teaching?* Sutton Trust. Accessed from https://www.suttontrust.com/our-research/great-teaching/ (accessed on 5/12/2023).
2 Coe, R., Aloisi, C, Higgins, S., and Elliot Major, L. *What Makes Great Teaching?*.
3 For example: Baumert, J., Kunter, M., Blum, W., Brunner, M., Voss, T., Jordan, A., Klusmann, U., Krauss, S., Neubrand, M., and Tsai, Y. (2010). Teachers' mathematical knowledge, cognitive activation in the classroom and student progress. *American Educational Research Journal*, 47(1), 133–180. Hill, H., Rowan, B., and Ball, D. (2005). Effects of teachers' mathematical knowledge for teaching on student achievement. *American Educational Research Journal*, 42(2), 371-406.
4 Coe, R., Aloisi, C, Higgins, S., and Elliot Major, L. *What Makes Great Teaching?*
5 Nathan, M., Alibali, M., and Koedinger, K. (2001). The expert blindspot – When content knowledge and pedagogical knowledge collide. Institute of Cognitive Science, Technical Report, Boulder, Colorado.
6 Wiliam, D. and Black, P. (1998). *Inside the Black Box – Raising Standards through Classroom Assessment*. https://kappanonline.org/inside-the-black-box-raising-standards-through-classroom-assessment/ (accessed 7/9/24).
7 Coe, R., Aloisi, C, Higgins, S., and Elliot Major, L. (2014). *What Makes Great Teaching?*
8 Benson, A., Li, D., and Shue, K. (2019). Promotions and the Peter principle. *The Quarterly Journal of Economics*, 134(4), 2085–2134.
9 Bravata, D. M., Watts, S. A., and Keefer, A. L. (2020). Prevalence, predictors, and treatment of impostor syndrome: A systematic review. *Journal of General Internal Medicine*, 35(4), 1252–1275.
10 For more on knowledge's role in developing expertise, see my first book *What Do New Teachers Need to Know?*

11 Stulberg, B. (2021). *The Practice of Groundedness*. London: Penguin.

12 Moon, A., Gan, M., and Critcher, C. R. (2020). The overblown implications effect. *Journal of Personality and Social Psychology*, 118(4), 720–742.

13 Kross, E. (2021). *Chatter*. London: Vermilion.

14 Interestingly, they also shortened the time periods people experienced positive emotions. 'Distancing shortened both negative and positive experiences... If you want to hold on to positive experiences, the last thing you want to do is become a fly on the wall. In such cases, immerse away.'.

15 O'Brien, E., and Kassirer, S. (2018). People are slow to adapt to the warm glow of giving. *Psychological Science*, 30(2), 193–204.

16 O'Brien, E., and Kassirer, S. People are slow to adapt to the warm glow of giving.

⚓ Ensuring Success – Notes for Leaders

One leader I spoke to was conscious of the responsibility of leadership. He said, 'When you're not at the coalface all the time, you have more time to think.' Leaders are busy people, equally concerned with balancing work and life as the teachers in their school. We shouldn't pretend, however, that leadership doesn't give us more freedom in the way that we work than a teacher with a full timetable. This leader was conscious of his 'luxury position' and the need to remember 'how difficult it can be at the coalface.' If we want our teachers to succeed, we need to understand their experience of the job. This understanding cannot be based on our assumptions or just on our own experience of the classroom; it must be grounded in real knowledge of the experience of those we lead.

Respect each individual teacher's understanding of success. Leaders know that successful teachers are the only possible foundation for a successful school. There is a tension, though, isn't there? If a teacher's idea of success is more time at home and less time at work, do we, as leaders, support that? Anxiety about that view of success reaching its logical conclusion is understandable. Equally, we might find ourselves in a situation where a new Head of MFL is needed. We have, in our view, the right candidate, an experienced member of the team. They work hard; they get great results; the children love their lessons. There's just one problem. Having asked them, we see clearly they don't want to do it.

Is it in a leader's interest, then, to accommodate such diverse aspirations from their teachers? Teachers have increased motivation for goals they have set themselves. We can try to direct or guide these goals, but we can't impose a goal that will have the same impact as one set by the individual.

Instead of trying to get teachers excited about goals we've forced upon them, perhaps we could create an ambitious vision of what we want our school to be. Staff need an idea of both where the school is going and how we're going to get there. They also need to feel that this is all doable and that they can be successful in that context. Experiencing success early drives us on towards more of it.

DOI: 10.4324/9781003453154-22

If we want teachers to do something we feel is vital to success of lessons or the school day, we should make reaching this success as easy as possible. If we want staff to use a new curriculum, plenty of time should be given to developing that curriculum but also developing teachers' ability to deliver it. If a new behaviour policy is chosen as the solution to a school's problems, staff need more than just the policy. They need it modelled and explored in training. They need leaders in classrooms supporting the implementation. They need supportive feedback from people who want them to succeed. A school leader's job, therefore, is to enable teachers they serve to be successful.

Mitigate the Peter Principle. Because the interview process in teaching is often high-stakes, expensive, and a bit risky, it's no wonder leaders are keen, where they can, to promote from within. Teachers you trust, ones you've worked with, whose classrooms you've been into, are surely just as capable as anyone you could appoint externally. Perhaps there's truth in this, but there's risk here too.

In reality, external appointments offer comparable risk. A candidate has been a strong teacher of KS2; we offer them Phase Leader. A candidate has led a successful English department; we offer them Assistant Headteacher. Previous success is what we put our trust in to make these decisions, and whilst it's better than previous failure or an absence of experience, such success is not a guarantee of similar achievements in a new job.

What can we do then? Only ever appoint a candidate who has direct experience of the job we're advertising? This doesn't feel realistic or practical. Instead, we could mitigate the effects of the Peter Principle at two crucial moments:

When Deciding to Appoint

Before rushing to appoint or promote, we should honestly evaluate the reasons why this specific person feels like a strong candidate to us. Where experience has already been gained or the person is already acting in the role, it makes sense to give the person the job. In situations less clearcut, we should ask:

- Has this candidate demonstrated experience similar to what they will be doing in the new job?

- Does the candidate have qualities or skills that will make a transition to a busier role/bigger team/more responsibilities easier?

Most schools probably have something like the above process. Senior leaders aren't universally rushing to appoint inexperienced or untested colleagues to positions of leadership. However, even if we ask ourselves the questions above, we can still be disappointed when a new leader doesn't live up to expectation. To understand another reason why that might be, let's turn to our second crucial moment.

When Inducting a New Leader

There's another question we can ask as we consider whether to appoint a candidate:

● Do we have the capacity to support this candidate to be successful in their induction (and beyond)?

This person's successes and failures in a new role aren't theirs alone. A school churning through leaders or a leadership team, constantly questioning the quality of new leaders, should spend time reflecting on whether they or their systems are the problem. A leadership position needs a more thorough induction than the instruction to read a few policies and know where to stand on duty.

Is a new leader inducted into *the way leaders act* in your school? Do they know how leaders respond when they witness unacceptable behaviour as they move around the site? Do they know how leaders chair meetings and run training sessions? Do they know how leaders give feedback to staff, praising and challenging what they witness?

Answers to these questions could be delivered in a meeting on a person's first day. They might be better received as a new leader shadows experienced colleagues and witnesses how leaders respond to the various situations that arise in any given school day.

Some schools tackle potential under-preparedness through a programme of training specifically designed for new leaders. Programmes like these can be uninspiring policy overload, or they can train staff in the systems and behaviours that will help teachers to be successful. It's worth seeking honest feedback on how new staff view these times to see whether our understanding of them matches with reality.

Create a culture of feedback. Teachers in your school shouldn't have to guess how they're doing. Imposter Syndrome festers in cultures of high accountability, low trust, and low feedback. Practices common in some schools exacerbate this culture:

● Regular learning walks where feedback is never given directly

● Lots of passive-aggressive reminders to all staff by email warning staff to stop or start something immediately

● An expectation that all teachers know something because it was said once in a meeting

● Requests to come to meetings with a leader without saying what the meeting is about

● Long lists of relatively arbitrary lesson guidelines (e.g., make sure the trust logo is on every slide, displays should look a certain way, every minute of the lesson is dictated in some way).

Instead of doing the above (and similar), we could create a culture of feedback by

- Making sure leaders are regularly in lessons

- Training leaders to give useful feedback

- Focusing on praise for the things going right by giving feedback one-to-one and celebrating successes as a group in meetings and briefings

- Regularly and, at least initially, gently challenging underperformance face to face

- Ensuring lesson observation is only ever supportive and developmental by removing any kind of grading from observation and focusing all feedback on developmental next steps.

Conclusion

One of my favourite things to do is have some friends round and play some board games. The more complex the rules of these games, the better. Boards are laid out. Strategies are formed. Alliances forged and then shattered. I suppose I like the feeling of being able to make decisions and plans within the structures of the game. I like knowing those structures well and using that knowledge to my advantage. I like getting to the end and the post-match analysis and argument.

Teaching isn't like a board game. The complexity of the classroom goes way beyond those games I love. And teaching isn't like a game in the sense in which we do serious work when we go to work in schools. It isn't frivolous. But teaching does present us with a series of challenges. There are structures within which we work. We can try a strategy or approach and watch it succeed or fail.

Teaching is also fun. Or it should be. As we look at the challenges of teaching, our aim will be to reduce the ability they hold to stop us doing our job well. We also want to deal with those challenges so that we can enjoy teaching. It's no good reducing workload if what we still have left to do is tedious and uninteresting. It's no good addressing the things that sap our motivation, if we forget what motivated us to teach in the first place.

When you start teaching, you enter a discourse *about* teaching that can shape your perspective in ways that are hard to shift. Ask a teacher how their day's going, and, invariably, it's full or busy or hectic. As teachers, we're in an incredibly noisy culture telling us we must work hard, be in a rush, go above and beyond, never stop, all to fulfil a vocation rather than a job. Of course, teachers are busy. Teachers *do* work hard. So hard that the questions *Could this be easier?* or *Could this be different?* are difficult to ask or to answer. But failing to ask or answer these questions can cause us to stall in poor habits or systems, unhappy where we are but unable to move forward. Failing to search for solutions to the problems we face, within both ourselves and those leading our schools, can leave us lost in difficult, joyless teaching.

When I look back at individual bits of advice from this book, I worry that they are too small to tackle the challenges of teaching. Those challenges are great, and

DOI: 10.4324/9781003453154-23

our solutions feel like they need to be massive to make a dent. I'd understand if at times you'd read this book and felt frustrated. *Just taking a break isn't going to help me... A to-do list won't shift the mountain I've got to get done... I'm already connected to my colleagues...* Remember, solutions can help you only when they address the problems you are trying to solve. And when it comes to change, small isn't necessarily weak.

Small and precise improvements can address the specific problems you are facing. Small is also doable. It's unlikely that you or your school is going to dramatically change overnight, but you can ask yourself:

- What are the problems getting in the way of being successful as a teacher?
- What are the problems that make teaching feel unsustainable to me?
- What options do I have to tackle these problems?
- What support can I access to help me tackle these problems?
- What can I start now? What do I want to invest more time in?

Teaching is, can be, and should be a joyful, emotional, intellectual pursuit. It can be all those things only if we are relentless in our removal of the obstacles in the way of that ideal. To be relentless, we can't simply look at the challenges of teaching. We must address the challenges of being a teacher.

Index

Printed in the United States
by Baker & Taylor Publisher Services